Table of Contents

Murders Unsolved: Cases That Have Baffled The Authorities For Years

Almost since the beginning of time, man has committed crimes that have defied our ability to explain. Among these are the most heinous crimes of all, murders. The taking of an innocent life goes against our most basic principles. Yet, murders continue to occur and sometimes they go unsolved.

Even with today's most innovative and groundbreaking technologies, not all criminals are caught. We hear that there is no such thing as the perfect crime. And undoubtedly, as our crime solving methods and abilities continue to advance, some currently unsolved crimes will be solved. But sometimes, it just doesn't happen.

Victim's families and friends are left never knowing the who and why of their loved one's passing. It is for their sake that law enforcement continues to work to solve these unsolved murders.

Following are some of the most famous and infamous cases that are still waiting. They are murders, unsolved.

The Fugitive's Wife - Marilyn Reese Sheppard

Victim: Marilyn Reese Sheppard
Date: July 3-4, 1954
Location: The Sheppard's home in Bay Village, Ohio
Suspects: The victim's husband, Dr. Samuel Sheppard, Richard Eberling, James Call, Esther and/or Spencer Houk

Backstory:
Marilyn Reese Sheppard had the perfect life. Aged thirty-one, she was a devoted wife and mother, and even taught Sunday school at church. Married to a neurosurgeon and with one son, the family lived in Bay Village, a quiet suburb of Cleveland. Her son, Chip, was seven when the incident occurred.

Marilyn was 5ft 7in, weighed 125 pounds, with brown hair and hazel eyes. She was described by her friends as beautiful, and was very much in love with her husband. She was also four months pregnant, though only close friends had been told.

Samuel Sheppard (known as Dr. Sam) and Marilyn had been childhood sweethearts. They met while still in high school and were married on February 21, 1945. Sam was the youngest of three boys, all who followed their father's footsteps and became doctors. He worked with all of them, dad included, at Bay View Hospital. His profession enabled their family to live comfortably, with a lakefront home.

On The Night in Question:
It was Saturday, the 3rd of July 1954. Sam had had a trying day. While at work, he had tried valiantly to save the life of a child who had been hit by a car. The

child did not survive, and it was likely that when he returned home, it was with a heavy heart.

That night, Sam and Marilyn were entertaining. Neighbors Don and Nancy Ahern were over for dinner. After they left, Marilyn reportedly went upstairs to bed, while Sam elected to watch a late night movie, eventually dozing off on the couch.

In the early morning, Sam awoke, reporting that he thought he heard his wife calling his name. When he entered their bedroom, he saw a form in the room. Before he could intervene, he was struck on the head from behind and knocked unconscious.

When he came to, he found his wife covered in blood. He checked for a pulse, but could find none. He then ran to the room next door, where their son Chip was sleeping, apparently unaware of all the fuss.

Hearing a noise downstairs, he followed and saw a person in his house. He gave chase and ended up on the beach. It's here Sam reports that he wrestled with the unidentified man, and was again knocked unconscious. When he awoke, he was laying outside, with half his body submerged in the lake.

He returned home, half thinking it had all been a terrible dream. Sam claims to not remember his exact actions from this point, but believes he examined his wife again, and may have visited other rooms. It was at that point that he called another neighbor, Bay Village Mayor Spencer Houk. It was 5:04am.

When Spencer and his wife arrived, they found Sam shirtless, and with a still wet bloodstain on his knee.

The police arrived soon after, to find Sam disoriented and in shock.

Curiously, the family dog was never heard to bark through the whole incident during the night, and their seven-year old son, sleeping in the next room over, was not disturbed.

During that morning, police, relatives, neighbors, and members of the press were all inside the home at some point. It was not sealed until later that afternoon. By then, Sam Sheppard had already been accused of the murder of his wife.

The Investigation:
The Sheppard's neighbors were the first to arrive on the scene. Spencer Houk reports that he ran upstairs, where he found Marilyn's body lying in the bedroom. The room was splattered with blood. Houk called the police at 5:57am.

Just after 6am on July 4, Bay Village patrolman Fred Drenkham arrived on the scene. Sam Sheppard was well known by the entire police department, as he was the police surgeon. He went straight upstairs, and could tell immediately that Marilyn was dead. She was almost unrecognizable, and blood drenched the bed.

After questioning Sam briefly, he told the Sheppard's friend and town mayor Spencer Houk that he felt it was a case beyond their capacity. Mayor Houk agreed, and called in the Cleveland police. An expert from their Scientific Investigation unit and two homicide detectives were assigned and sent out to the home. Although they usually only investigate crimes in rural towns, a sheriff from Cuyahoga County also arrived.

During this time, Sam Sheppard was taken by his brother to Bay View Hospital. At the same time, Spencer Houk disappeared, but returned after fifteen minutes, reporting that he had gone to lock his house. The Sheppard's son was then woken up and taken to his other uncle's house.

Shortly after, the house was crowded. Reporters were let into the house, as were concerned neighbors. Neighbors were also used to search the yard, during which time the mayor's son found Sam's medical bag in the bushes. It was opened and a number of personal objects were found inside. These too were handled and touched by a number of people before being turned over to the police.

Although a person in charge of the investigation was never formally named, from the beginning the press focused on the Coroner, Samuel R. Gerber, who arrived at 8am. He was a favourite of theirs, because he had a history of giving out information and good quotes that sold papers. At that point, he described the savagery of the attack to reporters, and also commented that there was no evidence of any break in attempt.

Shortly after, Geber visited Sam in hospital, along with the Bay Village chief of police. However, Geber questioned Sam on his own, without the chief of police in the room. Sam's injuries included a fractured vertebra, bruises, and chipped teeth. Geber took the clothes Sam had been wearing, and then returned to the scene. Here, he recounted the recent interview to the reporters.

The two detectives from Cleveland finished examining the scene, and then went to the hospital to also question Sam, but he had been sedated. So, they returned to the house and began questioning the neighbors. They then returned again to question Sam, though he would later refer to it as more of a grilling, asking questions about all parts of his life, including relationships with other women.

Crime was usually unknown in the Bay Village area, and the town had a reputation for its safety. People were finding Sam's recount of being knocked unconscious by an unknown intruder hard to believe. Why was there no evidence in the house of a break in or third party, and why was the couple's son not disturbed nor did their dog bark?

That evening, a well-known criminal attorney, William Corrigan, visited Sam while he was still in the hospital, and this too was reported in the papers the next morning. Unknown to the public at the time, the Cleveland detectives had recommended Sam's arrest for his wife's murder.

The police also had an independent doctor examine Sam. He reported that Sam had suffered a serious injury to his spinal cord in his neck, and was also lacerated and bruised on his face.

Four days after the murder, on Tuesday July 7, Sam attended Marilyn's funeral, and was in great distress during the eulogy. By then, detectives were making complaints about Sam's brother and doctor, who were apparently preventing them from interviewing Sam. Geber reported to the press that the family was not co-operating. Sam, growing concerned with how the tide seemed to be turning against him, announced a $10,000 reward for the capture of the killer. He also denied he had ever refused to talk to police.

Sam was then taken back to the house by detectives on July 8, where he found news photographers and public spectators camped on the lawn. He told police he wanted them off his property, but they were not removed. On the same day, he made his first public interview. This, along with the reporter's coverage of the tour of the house, was all in the papers in great detail.

Sam's criminal attorney also allowed Sam to be questioned by police, without his attorney being present. It became clear that he was the prime suspect, and the public was starting to talk about how Sam's supposed reticence to talk to police or to take a lie detector test was evidence of guilt.

There were hundreds of calls from the public to police regarding the matter, and the police did also question other suspects, but they were all released without charge. Two unrelated people reported seeing a man near the home at the time of the attack, while others reported lights on in the house, contradicting Sam's story.

The police finally closed the home to all but officials, but the scene was already well and truly compromised.

From the beginning, the entire case was influenced by the media. At first, they reported the tragedy of the family and the horror that something could happen to such a lovely couple. But, the tide soon turned. Multiple editorials ran front page. Many were later shown to include incorrect or inadmissible information. The local media ran stories that included facts that were either non-existent or disproved. During the trial, a radio show aired a report about a woman from New York who claimed to be Sam Sheppard's lover and mother of his illegitimate child; neither of the claims was true.

On July 21, 1954, the Cleveland Press ran a front-page article calling for a public inquest. Just a few hours later Geber announced he was calling one the very next day. The inquest was held in a gym and was open to the public, reporters, and live television and radio crews. Sam Sheppard was searched in full view of the entire crowd, and his own lawyer was forbidden from participating as Geber ruled it was not an official court proceeding. When Sam's lawyer tried to introduce evidence of his own, he was removed entirely. At no time did he advise Sam of his Fifth Amendment rights.

The inquest also formally introduced evidence that Sam had allegedly been cheating on his wife with Susan Hayes, a former Bay View Hospital nurse who now lived in Los Angeles. Susan talked to police and the press herself, all the while headlines accusing Sam of lying and editorials of his sure guilt continued to be published.

On July 23, the Cleveland police took over the case, and by July 30 the Cleveland Press again ran a front page story titled "Why isn't Sam Sheppard in Jail?" Sam was arrested that very night. Reporters and the public were again present at the arrest. When Corrigan tried to visit Sam in jail, he was denied access. Without a break, Sam was questioned for over twelve hours by the police. He maintained his story, and after three days they finally gave up. Gradually the reports of the case faded from the front page, for the time being.

Suspects:

Although there were no other suspects publically named before Sam Sheppard's own arrest, after his trial, other suspects became known. One was Richard Eberling, a handyman and window washer who was hired by the Sheppards. A ring that had once been owned by Marilyn was found in his possession, which he stole from another family member after her murder. Later, his DNA was compared with blood from Marilyn's crime scene, but the results were inconclusive. Eberling claimed he had cut himself while working at the house, but perhaps this was an attempt to cover up involvement in the murder. Another witness named Vern Lund signed an affidavit in 1954, when he was dying of cancer, that it was he and not Eberling who had washed the windows in the house.

Most surprisingly, in 1998, DNA evidence tested from a vaginal swab taken from Marilyn in 1954 matched Eberling's DNA, as well as that of a second man's. This is however in dispute due to degradation of the evidence over time. Controversial evidence reports tool marks near the basement door, and other evidence of a break in. However, later reports indicate that the basement door merely lead to a crawl space.

Eberling died in prison in 1998, serving a life sentence for another murder, committed in 1984.

After Sam Sheppard's own case was finally complete, it then came to light that Sheppard's lawyer, F. Lee Bailey, thought that guilt lay with Esther Houk, the wife of the Bay Village Mayor. Claims were made that either Esther Houk was having an affair with Sam, or that indeed Spencer Houk was the one having the affair! A burglary was then faked to cover up the murder. Some theories also state that it was Spencer who attacked Sam, having tried to flee to his house along the beach. Under hypnosis, Sam had later said that he remembered the attacker to have a limp, which Spencer Houk also had.

In April 2002, a former FBI agent who had become an author released a book titled *Tailspin: The Strange Case of Major Call*. The author, Bernard F. Connors, claimed James Call was a pilot in the Air Force in 1954, from which he went AWOL. According to the book, at that time Call visited his sister in Manua, Ohio, a town thirty minutes away from Bay Village. It also reports that he was a known burglar, who had killed a New York policeman during a previous robbery. It was said that he carried a luger pistol and a crowbar, and also walked with a limp. Call did not have an alibi for the date of Marilyn's murder, and he had been picked up as a hitchhiker the day after. The driver reported that he had blood on his shoes. He was also identified as closely resembling the man that original witnesses reported seeing hanging about the Sheppard home just before the murder. Call himself was killed in a car accident in 1970.

The Trial:

At 9am on October 18, 1954, the case of State of Ohio vs. Sam H. Sheppard was called. Multiple reporters were allowed in the courtroom. The names and addresses of the jurors had even been published in the papers. The trial heard several witnesses, the most damning of which was the coroner. Gerber claimed that in a bloodstain on the pillowcase, he could see the impression of a surgical instrument. However, when pushed he could not identify the particular instrument, nor had he recovered any that matched the mark. Susan Hayes was also called. She testified that she had been involved in an affair with Sam Sheppard, and that he had wanted a divorce from his wife.

Throughout the trial, the jury was not sequestered, and several of them admitted hearing radio broadcasts about the case, but they were not dismissed and substituted. Years later, jurors have said it is likely they were influenced by the press, both before and during the trial. Reporters even travelled with the jurors to visit the scene of the crime, and the jury was never questioned about anything they heard from the media.

Officials involved in the case, including police and the judge, all gave media interviews while the trial was still ongoing. One reporter would later mention that the judge from the first trial called Sheppard 'guilty as hell' while he was still deliberating over the trial.

The jury was finally sequestered for deliberations, but even then they were allowed to make unmonitored phone calls to their families.

After 100 hours of deliberation, Sam Sheppard was found guilty of second-degree murder. The judge passed an immediate sentence of life in prison, over Corrigan's objections. Soon after the trial, Sheppard's mother committed suicide. Eleven days after that, his father died of a hemorrhaging gastric ulcer.

Meanwhile, Corrigan began working on an appeal for a new trial. It was to be the first of twelve unsuccessful attempts. On July 20, 1961, William Corrigan died, having never won a new trial for Sam Sheppard.

After Corrigan's death, at the request of Sheppard's family, F. Lee Bailey took over the case and continued the appeal process. Finally, on July 16, 1964, his writ of habeas corpus was granted by a US district court judge. The trial in 1954 was referred to as a 'mockery of justice' and the state of Ohio was ordered to release Sheppard on bond. They gave prosecutors sixty days to bring new charges against Sam, or the case would be dismissed permanently.

However, in May of 1965 a federal appeals court voted to reinstate Sheppard's conviction. He was however allowed to remain free while waiting for his appeal to the U.S. Supreme Court. The justices agreed to hear the case, and it was set for February 1968. On July 6, they delivered their ruling. The Supreme Court found that Sheppard's due process had been denied, and twelve years after that fateful night, Sam Sheppard was legally an innocent man. However, he still had to face a second trial.

Determined to avoid the same fate as the judge from the first trial, the judge assigned to the second trial,

Francis Talty, forbade any media from having tables inside the bar. No one could leave or enter while court was in session, and no one was to make any statements to the press. He limited the number of spectators and reporters, and he determined which media would be given seats. This time, the jury was sequestered, and their phone calls and access to media was monitored. On November 1, 1966, the trial began.

Sheppard's lawyer took a different tack with questioning witnesses, and many who had given extensive testimony during the first trial were quickly dismissed. He also got William Geber to admit the impression in the blood of the pillowcase could have been as simple as a pair of pliers.

The jury started deliberations just after lunch on November 16. By 9:30pm that night, they had a verdict – not guilty.

Current Status of Case:
After the trial, Sam Sheppard returned to medicine, but left after he was sued for malpractice in the death of a patient. He had married his second wife during the appeals, but divorced in 1968. He married once more in 1969, though no documentation of the marriage has been found. Sam moved to Columbus, and for a while had a career as a pro wrestler.

Dr. Sam Sheppard died at age 46, on April 6, 1970, of liver failure due to heavy drinking.

As he grew up, Sam Reese Sheppard, Sam and Marilyn's son, became an advocate for his father's case, and wanted his father to be declared innocent, rather than just not guilty. Sam had his father exhumed for a DNA comparison of trial evidence. Dr. Sam was then reburied next to Marilyn.

In December 1998, the Ohio Supreme Court ruled the case could go forward. The 'third trial' started January 21, 2000, after Sam Sheppard had already been dead for thirty years. As it was a civil trial, no majority was needed and the burden of proof had changed.

On March 13, the case went to the jury, and they were back in less than three hours. They found that Sam Sheppard was 'not innocent', as put by the media. The verdict was appealed, but on February 22, 2002 a three-judge panel of the Eighth District Court of Appeals rejected this too. They appealed again, to the Ohio Supreme Court, but they refused to hear the case.

The extremely popular TV show, *The Fugitive*, is believed by most to be inspired by the case of Marilyn Sheppard, though this has officially been denied. Ratings of the show declined after Sheppard was found not guilty, and the show was since cancelled.

The case of the murder of Marilyn Sheppard remains officially unsolved.

America's Unknown Child – The Boy in the Box

Victim: Name Unknown
Date: February 25, 1957
Location: Fox Chase, Philadelphia, Pennsylvania
Suspects: The mother of "M", Mrs. Margaret Martinez, Private Edward J. Posivak

Backstory:
The boy in the box is a name given to an unidentified murder victim, who was found lying in a cardboard box in the Fox Chase section of Philadelphia on February 25, 1957. His body was naked and battered. He was approximately four to six years old at the time of his death.

On The Day in Question:
The person who eventually reported the boy's body was not actually the first to find it. The first person to find the boy in the box was a young man who had placed muskrat traps, and was checking in on them. The young man worried that his traps would be confiscated by the police, and so he kept quiet on the grisly find.

A couple of days later, a college student driving past saw a rabbit running through the thickets.
He knew that traps had been set in the area, and so he pulled over, followed and found the body. He also didn't want to get involved, and so he waited until the following day to finally report what he'd found.

The body was wrapped in a plaid blanket, and placed inside a box that had once held a baby's bassinet purchased from J.C. Penney's. The boy was clean and dry, and recently groomed. However, he looked to be undernourished. Clumps of hair found on the body suggested he had been groomed after death.

The boy had many bruises on his body, particularly on his head and face, and all appeared to have been inflicted at the same time. He also had seven scars on his body, some of which could have been surgical in nature. Two were on the chest and groin. X-Rays showed no evidence of fractures at any time in his life.

When examined, one eye fluoresced under UV light, which indicated that eye drops may have been used. Perhaps the child had a chronic eye condition. He had not eaten in the two to three hours before he died, and his hands and feet were wrinkled, as if they had been submerged in water for some time.

Establishing a time of death was made difficult due to the cool weather. The boy could have been lying in his box for anywhere from a couple of days to two or three weeks.

About fifteen feet from the box, a distinctive blue cap was found.

The Investigation:
The case attracted a huge following in the media, and the boy's photo was also put into every gas bill posted in Philadelphia. Thousands of posters printed with his photo and description were displayed all over Philadelphia and also distributed across the country. The police even dressed the boy's body and posed him in a chair, thinking that a more natural setting of the body may jog somebody's memory.

The box was examined, but no fingerprints were found. The police also checked records against the boy's own fingerprints, but no match was found.

The blue hat found at the scene was recognized as being made by a local, a Mrs. Hannah Robbins. She recalled that a man aged between twenty-six and thirty had bought it, but had requested that she add a leather strap and a buckle to it. He was in working clothes, had no discernible accent, and he was alone. The man had not been seen since, and no one remembered seeing a boy wearing the cap.

Bill Kelly, a fingerprint expert, took the footprints of the boy in the box on the day he was found, but no match was found at local hospitals. Over the years, he has on his own time, compared the footprints of every birth in each nearby hospital, but he has never found a match.

In 1965, Kelly had an idea that perhaps the boy had been a recent immigrant, which would explain why he had no footprints or hospital records on file. He discovered a boy who looked exactly like the boy in the box, who was from a Hungarian family. However, upon investigation the boy was found safe and well.

At the time of the discovery, the police checked every orphanage, foster home and hospital in the area when the body was found, but no one reported a child missing. Early leads included a New York Airman, who thought it was his kidnapped son, a boy from West Philly thinking it was his younger brother, and a woman from Lancaster who thought it was her son, who was being looked after by his (in her mind) unfit father. These and all other leads were eventually proven false.

Like most unsolved cases, there are a huge number of theories surrounding the boy in the box. There is however two most investigated.

Remington Bristow was an employee of the medical examiner's office, who was obsessed with the case. He investigated on his own right up until his own death in 1993. In 1960, he contacted a psychic from New Jersey. Approximately 1.5 miles from the site where the body was recovered was a foster home. The psychic described to Bristow a home that matched the foster home. In addition, when she was brought to visit the site, she led him directly to the home.

Bristow went to an estate sale being held at the foster home, and found a baby's bassinette that was similar to the one that had been sold at J.C. Penny at the time. He also found blankets that were similar to the one the boy was found wrapped in. Bristow believed that the boy in the box was the child of a stepdaughter of the man who ran the foster home. He theorizes that after the accidental death of the boy, they got rid of the body so she would not be exposed as a single mother.

However, police were never able to find any evidence to link the family to the boy, and a DNA test has since also ruled out the daughter as the child's mother.

The second major theory only came to light in February 2002, and involves a woman who is only identified as "M". "M" claims that her mother purchased the boy from his birth parents in the summer of 1954. She reports that her mother was abusive, and that the boy was named Jonathan.

According to "M", the boy was then a victim of extreme physical and sexual abuse for two and a half years, and that her mother killed him in a rage by slamming him into the floor after he vomited in the bath. She reported that her mother then cut his long hair in an attempt to disguise him, and dumped the body. Police had noted that the boy appeared to have an unprofessional haircut, and bruises around his hairline.

"M" claims that while they were dumping the boy, a man driving past pulled over and offered his assistance just as they were preparing to remove the boy's body from the trunk. They declined the offer, and after awhile the man drove off. This statement matches original witness testimony from 1957, which alleged that the body was not transported in the box, but it was simply found at the scene and used.

Police considered that the story was plausible, but were troubled by reports that "M" had a history of mental illness. They interviewed neighbors, who reported that there had never been a young boy living with "M" and her claims were ridiculous.

Suspects:
Despite never identifying the boy, there were some suspects that were examined by police. A Mrs. Margaret Martinez, from Thornton, Colorado was arrested in 1960, after she admitted to throwing the body of her three-year old daughter into a trashcan. She matched the description of a woman who had

been seen standing next to a parked car near where the body was found, but questioning never revealed any connection or link to the boy in the box.

Private Edward J. Posivak, from Philadelphia, was detained by police after the disappearance of a woman he was dating. Police found clippings about the boy in the box case in his car. However, the Private agreed to take a lie detector test and passed. He was questioned extensively, but detectives were convinced in the end he was not anywhere nearby when the crime took place.

Six people originally identified the boy as Terry Lee Speece, an eight year old who lived with his roofer and laborer father. Police issued a twelve state alarm to find his father, even though the boy's mother (who had not seen him for a year) and Terry's maternal grandparents said that the boy in the box was not Terry. Sometime later, Terry was found alive and living with his father in Ardmore, PA.

Many other leads over the years have also proved fruitless.

Current Status of Case:
The case is one of the more well known unsolved mysteries, and has been featured on *America's Most Wanted*. It has also been fictionalized on shows such as *Cold Case*, *CSI: Crime Scene Investigation* and *Law & Order: SVU*.

In 1998, the boy was exhumed and DNA evidence was collected. He was then reburied as America's Unknown Child in a donated coffin in Ivy Hill cemetery. Efforts are currently underway to try to match DNA extracted from one of his teeth to any living relative. Unfortunately however, the sample sequence is likely too small to ever provide a conclusive match to anyone.

The chances are that anyone who was involved in the case, or indeed committed the murder, is now also dead. Many believe that had the crime occurred in modern times, it would have been solved.

Gruesome Inspiration - Lake Bodom Murders

Victims: Seppo Boisman, Anja Maki, Maili Bjorklund
Date: June 5, 1960
Location: Lake Bodom, Espoo, Finland
Suspects: Pauli Loma, Pentti Soininen, Valdemar Gyllstrom, Hans Assmann,
           Nils Wilhelm Gustafsson

Backstory:
The victims of this unsolved mystery were Finnish teenagers Seppo Antero Boisman (18), his girlfriend Anja Tuulikki Maki (15) and Maili Irmeli Bjorklund (15). Her boyfriend, Nils Wilhelm Gustafsson (18) survived the attack, but was injured. Nothing much is known about the four teenagers before their infamous deaths. Even their graves at the St. Lawrence churchyard in Uusimaa, Finland show no birthdates.

On The Day in Question:
Lake Bodom is near the Espoo, a city in Finland. The town is about 22 kilometers (approximately 13 miles) from Helsinki, the capital and largest city of Finland.

On June 5, 1960, the four teenagers went camping on the lake's shoreline. Between 4 and 6am, an unknown person murdered three by stabbing them to death, and left the last wounded with a blunt instrument. Nils Wilhelm Gustafsoon was found alive, and suffered a concussion, fractured jaw, facial bone fractures, and facial bruising.

A carpenter who was walking through the scene at 11am the next morning alerted police. They found a slashed tend with a groaning young man lying on top of it, and then three dead bodies.

24

The tent was not in a smart spot, pitched on a slight slope in the shade. The boy's motorcycles leaned up against a nearby tree. Seppo had gotten the tent from work, and had also procured alcohol from his workmates. Finally, he also had condoms that he'd gotten from the black market.

It had been a warm day, but it's not known if the teens went swimming or fished at the lake. They went inside the tent at 10:30pm. The tent was small, and the boys lay in the middle with the girls on the outsides. Because of Finland's location on the globe, the sun rose at 3:06am that day. A long summer's day can last for nearly 19 hours. The murders happened between 4 and 6am, and police were on the scene at noon.

The Investigation:
Police discovered that someone else had found the crime scene before the carpenter reported it later that morning. At 6am, some boys who were bird watching saw the collapsed tent, but their attention was captured by the sight of the motorcycles instead. They mistook the person lying on top of the tent as simply sunbathing. They think that they saw a fair-haired person walking away from the tent.

A blond man was also seen by another boy who was fishing at a nearby inlet, but the man's identify remains a mystery.

The sole survivor, Gustafsson reported that the attacker was clad totally in black, and with bright red eyes. He was reported to be in a state of shock.

No murder weapon was ever found at the site, but some of the teenagers' belongings were reported as missing. A search of the lake failed to reveal any further evidence.

Suspects:
Many suspects were questioned and investigated over the course of the investigation.

Pauli Loma had escaped from a work department near to the scene. He was soon caught by police and was questioned over the murders. However, he was able to provide an alibi to police.

A maintenance worker named Pentti Soininen had been convicted of a string of both property crimes and violent crimes in the late 1960's. When he was in jail at age 24 over another matter, he confessed to being the Lake Bodom murderer. The police discovered that he had lived close to the site at the time of the crime, and investigated, but in the end his admissions were not believed. Soininen was mentioned to have a psychopathic personality, and could be very evasive, especially when affected by drugs and alcohol. Soininen had a long history of crime, including theft, assault, and robbery. He hanged himself in a prisoner transport station in 1969.

Valdemar Gyllstrom, who worked in a kiosk near the lake, became a prime suspect in the murders. People reported his hatred of campers at the lake, and that he was often aggressive towards them. In 1969, he himself drowned in the lake, and neighbors then reported that he had confessed to killing the teens when he was drunk.

Police searched his home and found no evidence relating to the case, but it was revealed that a couple of days after the murders, he had filled in a well in his courtyard. His relatives have since reported they believe the murder weapons are buried there.

At the time, his wife gave him an alibi, but after his death she recanted and said that he threatened to kill her if she had ever told the truth.

Finally, there is the theory of Hans Assmann. An alleged KGB spy, he came into the Helsinki Surgical Hospital on the 6th of June 1960. He was behaving very strangely, and was in a disheveled state. His fingernails were black, and his clothing was covered in red marks. His behavior was very odd, acting both nervous and aggressive.

Assmann's clothing matches the earlier descriptions of the murderer, and it was revealed that he had cut off his long blond hair, after those details emerged to the public. At the time, he lived within 5 kilometers (approximately 3 miles) from Bodom.

Hospital staff noted that his behavior at the time could be suggestive of guilt, and that the stains on his clothing were most likely blood. However, the police never collected them for testing. Assmann has since been linked to other unsolved homicides in Finland.

The Trial:
The sole survivor, Nils Wilhelm Gustafsson, went on to lead a normal life until almost forty four years after the original crime. Police arrested Gustafsson in March 2004. In early 2005, the Finnish National

Bureau of Investigation announced that they had solved the case, based on new blood stain analysis.

They announced that Gustafsson had attacked his friends in a jealous rage over Bjorklund. She had been stabbed repeatedly after the strike that killed her, while the others were killed with less savagery. Gustafsson's own injuries were also lesser.
On August 4, 2005, the trial got underway. The prosecution asked for life in prison. The defense argument was that the murder was the work at least one outsider, possibly more, and given the extent of Gustafsson's own injuries, it would have been impossible for him to kill three other people.

Gustafsson was acquitted of all charges on October 7, 2005. Finland state also paid him €44,900 for mental suffering, caused by his long time in jail before the trial.

Current Status of Case:
The Lake Bodom murder case remains unsolved. Every year, numerous amateur detectives scour the bottom of the lake with metal detectors, but no murder weapon has ever been found.

A Finnish death metal band, whose members come from Espoo named their group Children of Bodom, after the lake and the unsolved murders.

Money, Mystery and Murder - Helen Brach

Victim: Helen Voorhees Brach
Date: February 17, 1977
Location: Mayo Clinic, Rochester, Minnesota, O'Hare Airport, Chicago, Illinois
Suspects: Jack Matlick, Richard Bailey, Joe Plemmons, Ken Hansen, hit-man Curt

Backstory:
Helen Voorhees Brach was born on November 10, 1911. The coat check girl at the Palm Beach Country Club, this was where she met her husband Frank Brach, a part of the E.J. Brach & Sons Candy Company. Soon after divorcing his first wife, he proposed to Helen, and they were married in 1950, when she was 39 years old.

An animal lover, Helen is reported to have been generous to a fault. The couple lived in Chicago, and spent winters in Florida. Helen was seen as being a little eccentric by her friends. She was interested in the spirit world, and became heavily involved in animal rights, particularly later in life. She had a funny habit of worrying about relatively small charges, such as a $100 rise in rent, while at the same time lavishly spending much more on family and friends.

Frank Brach died in 1970, leaving Helen a multimillionaire widow. Her worth was $20 million.

On The Day in Question:
On February 17, 1977, Helen had undergone a routine medical checkup at the Mayo Clinic, in Rochester, Minnesota. Doctors there pronounced her

fit and well. After leaving the clinic, she went to catch a return flight home to Chicago.

A gift shop attendant near the clinic reports Brach as saying "I'm in a hurry, my houseman is waiting'. This was the last time an independent witness saw Helen alive. When later questioned, the attendant is sure Helen used these words, even though she was travelling alone.

The crew of the commercial flight she was supposed to return home on did not remember seeing her on the flight. This was a little strange, as Helen was not easy to miss, due to her status and the way she carried herself. However, they were interviewed some time later, and so memories may have been forgotten or vague.

Helen's houseman and chauffer, Jack Matlick, reported to police that he picked Helen up at O'Hare Airport, and that Helen then went home. Four days later he dropped her back at O'Hare for a flight to Florida. Helen was known to her friends as a 'telephone addict', and yet she did not make a single call during those four days. He also says that she was dropped at O'Hare three hours early, and that she had no luggage. No one has seen Helen since.

Matlick was a long-term employee of Helen and her husband. After Frank's death, he stayed on to help Helen around the household. When police investigated, there was no evidence of them being anything other than employer-employee.

When police started an investigation into her disappearance, they had no idea what a Pandora's box they were opening. The investigation eventually spun into charges of arson and fraud, involving a number of people.

The Investigation:
Jack Matlick waited two weeks to report Helen missing. When he did, he was told by police that the report had to come from a family member. Then and only then did he tell anyone in Helen's family of her disappearance. Matlick informed Helen's brother Charles Voorhees.

Matlick was on the police's radar from the beginning. They discovered that he had cashed checks supposedly written by Brach. When police investigations revealed the signature to be a forgery, he claimed that Helen had injured her hand and had to sign with her left. In his defense, investigations revealed that he had not written the checks either.

In the four days between when he claimed he had picked her up, and then dropped her back at the airport, a room at Helen's home had been completely repainted and re-carpeted. However, workmen reported seeing nothing unusual in the room.

That weekend, Matlick also purchased a small meat grinder attachment for a blender. Police investigated, but it was later determined that it was too small to be used for the disposal of human remains.

Matlick didn't normally live at the house when Helen was home. However, that weekend his wife recalled that he had told her he was staying there as he had work to do. He told authorities that Helen had stayed in that weekend to prepare for her Florida trip, but friends who had stopped by were told by the houseman that Helen was not available.

Years later, Matlick's wife told police that he had actually called her on February 17, 1977 and told her that Helen hadn't returned from the Mayo Clinic, and so he was going to stay at the house and wait for her.

Helen kept very detailed journals, but had also left instructions for them to be burned if anything should ever happen to her. Strangely, before he had even gone to police once he knew of Helen's disappearance, Helen's brother gave Matlick permission to burn the journals, along with many of Helen's personal papers. No doubt these contained important evidence that was now lost.

Police turned to Helen's trip to Florida. Helen usually travelled with multiple trunks of clothing, and was a late sleeper, rarely up early. It would therefore have been very unusual for her to show up at the airport without luggage, and to be there at 7am, three hours before her flight boarded. Matlick was given a lie detector test, and passed.

The police eventually gave up. However, in the spring of 1977, the investigation was re-opened. A dispute over who should be the administrator of her estate in her absence was ongoing, and the judge therefore appointed John Cadwallander Menk, a former head of the Chicago Bar Association, to investigate her disappearance. He was instructed to 'get inside her head' so to determine how she would want her money spent. Helen Brach had left over $20 million behind when she disappeared.

A three-year investigation revealed nothing, however this is where the name Richard Bailey was first mentioned in relation to Helen and her affairs.

In May of 1984, Helen Brach was declared dead. Charles Voorhees, Helen's brother, did very well out of the will.

Then, in 1989, the US Attorney's office started an investigation into a case of fraud involving horses. It didn't take long for Richard Bailey, and then Helen Brach's names to emerge.

Suspects:
Although Jack Matlick had been quickly under police suspicion, his case did not go any further. It was discovered that he was also an ex-con, but without solid evidence the police and prosecutors saw an unwinnable case and did not proceed. Matlick always maintained his claim of innocence, and denied to reporters over the years that he knew what happened to Helen.

Although not even on the police's radar at the time of her disappearance, the investigation into fraud by the U.S. Attorney's office linked Richard Bailey intimately to Helen Brach. Bailey targeted rich women in a number of cons using horses. He would romance the women, and then convince them to either buy a dud or overvalued racing horse, in cahoots with partners in the fraud to act as the horse sellers. When there was no more money to be had, he'd quickly end the relationship.

It was revealed that Helen and Bailey had been in a relationship since 1973, and in 1975 he sold her horses worth less than $20,000 for $98,000, as well as a group of breeding mares. It seems that Helen had become suspicious, for she confided in a friend, and that friend was going to accompany her to the State Attorney's office to report Richard Bailey's activities as soon as she returned from the Mayo Clinic.

The Trial:
By 1989, the US Attorney's investigation had turned up evidence of criminal activity by associates of Richard Bailey. He was charged with conspiracy, and named with several others (although he was not formally charged) in a plot to kill Helen Brach. However, even Helen's brother questioned if he was really the guilty party. It took about five years, but in 1994 they finally had enough evidence to take Richard Bailey, along with more than twenty other defendants, to a federal grand jury.

In July, Bailey was indicted on twenty-nine counts, including the murder of Helen Brach. Rather than risk a jury, Bailey pleaded guilty to the fraud counts, betting that the murder charge would then be thrown out by the judge due to lack of evidence. Bailey bet wrong. The judge gave Bailey a life sentence, and made it clear that as well as being for his fraud offences, it also reflected evidence that he was involved in a conspiracy to kill Helen. He also added on a fine of $1 million.

Bailey's sentence was later reduced to 30 years, however Bailey was now 67 years old and so he was likely to still be in jail until the end of his life.

However, that was just the beginning. During the investigation into Helen's murder, authorities were able to solve a string of homicides that dated back as far as 1955. They involved a man who was suspected of also being involved in Helen's murder.

In all, thirty-three convictions were made on a range of charges, from arson, fraud, and obstruction of justice, all from the investigation into her disappearance and the horse fraud case.

Helen's body has never been found.

Current Status of Case:
Under threat of legal action for allegedly stealing $100,000 worth of gold coins from Helen's home, Jack Matlick relinquished a shared in her estate that had been left to him in her will. He died in a Pennsylvania nursing home on February 14, 2001, aged 79 years old.

After Matlick's death, a former federal agent who worked on the case came forward and said that Matlick was indeed responsible for Helen's death. Helen's brother also believes Matlick to be the guilty party.

Because her body has not been found, there can be no burial for Helen Brach. Her dogs however are interred in her mausoleum with her husband.

In early 2005, Richard Bailey's attorney, Kathleen Zellner, filed a brief to argue for a new sentence hearing. On March 21, 2005 the Seventh Circuit of Appeals rejected his request for a new sentencing hearing. Bailey claimed that he had new evidence proving that he was innocent of the murder conspiracy, but the court disagreed.

An unnamed informant had apparently confessed involvement in Helen's murder to the Federal Bureau of Alcohol, Tobacco, and Firearms. He had said that Bailey had nothing to do with Helen's murder.

The affidavit said that Helen had either been beaten or strangled, and then dumped in a white-hot steel furnace near Gary, Indiana. The witness, who had been granted immunity, said that Helen was picked up and returned to Chicago by car on that fateful day, and a stand-in caught her flight back. She had been killed because she was scheduled to meet with authorities over the horse trading fraud case.

In the end, the witness turned out to be Joe Plemmons, a man who had testified at Bailey's own trial that Bailey had once tried to hire him to kill Helen. He said that he had been forced to kill her by being held at gunpoint himself. He named Ken Hansen, the man who had been imprisoned for the other killings from 1955, and a hit-man named Curt, as the perpetrators.

The final word to kill Helen came from another insider in the horse trade, and not Bailey. Joe Plemmons was in possession of a ring that he claims belonged to Helen, which he kept after it fell off her finger when he was disposing of her body. Helen's family and friends have identified it as hers, but DNA testing was not able to prove it.

Bailey's appeal was denied on the basis that it did not prove he was not complicit in Helen's murder. Without being implicated in killing her, Bailey would have only served around 11 years for the fraud case.

Over the years, there have been reports that Oliver Stone plans to make a movie about Helen's disappearance and the investigations that all stemmed from it. Whatever happened to Helen Brach, It Is highly likely she would be have died a natural death by now had she somehow survived back in the 1970's, simply of old age.

Friendly Fire? - Raymond Washington, founder of the Crips

Victims: Raymond Lee Washington
Date: August 9, 1979
Location: The corner of 64th and San Pedro, Los Angeles, Claifornia
Suspects: None

Backstory:
Raymond Lee Washington was born on August 14, 1953 in Los Angeles, California. He was the original founder of the South Central Los Angeles gang the Crips.

Born to Violet Samuel and Reginald Washington, he had three older brothers and a younger half brother. His parents divorced when he was two. Raymond was raised by his mother and stepfather, growing up on East 76th Street.

As a teen, Raymond was constantly in trouble with the police. His mother said that he didn't go out of his way to find trouble, but that he would always defend himself if approached, and that he also tried to protect the community. However, neighbors referred to him as a bully.

Raymond's friends reported that he was a good football player, but that he never played in school due to poor grades. He often transferred between schools due to multiple expulsions.

Meanwhile, in the late 1960's, youth crime was escalating in and around the Watts area of Los Angeles. Old gangs had been ended by activist groups such as the Black Panthers, and new gangs began to spring up in their place.

In his early teens, Raymond joined the Avenues gang. At 15 years old, he had a fight with the then leader's younger brother. In retaliation, the leader of the gang beat up Raymond, and Raymond left the gang.

Then, in late 1968, Raymond organized a group of other kids from the neighborhood and formed the Baby Avenues, emulating an older group called the Avenue Boys, a gang since 1964. They then became the Avenue Cribs.

Raymond disliked guns and knives, and believed that fist fighting was the most effective way to resolve differences. This however changed in his gang by the time of his death. Raymond was the best fighter in the gang, and was feared by fellow members. His original plan had been to secure the local area and protect his friends from more dangerous gangs, but his own gang soon became a haven for violence from within.

By 1969, the gang was going by the name of simply Crips. This is still the name they use today, and they are now one of the largest and most notorious gangs in the United States.

In 1974, Raymond, then 19 years old, was arrested for second-degree robbery, and sentenced to five years in prison. Once inside, he began to recruit for his gang. This angered established black gangs inside the prison.

While he was still in prison, fellow Crips members on the outside murdered a rival gang member. The gang member had relatives inside the prison, and they held Raymond responsible. He became a target and they tried to kill him in prison, but he survived.

When he was released in the 1970's, the Crips were involved in a gang war and had escalated to include the regular use of guns. Raymond hated this, and implored his members to abandon them, but they refused.

Ultimately, Raymond started to distance himself from the gang. He wanted to bring all the new offshoot gangs back into one unified group, and stop the infighting. He also wanted to make a truce with the other gang in the war, the Bloods. None of this sat well with fellow members.

On The Night in Question:
On the evening of August 9, 1979, at around 10pm, Raymond was hanging out on the corner of 64th and San Pedro in Los Angeles, when a car pulled up and an unidentified occupant called him over to the car. Witnesses report that Washington seemed to know the other person, and he started talking to the person in the car.

The person in the car then drew a sawn off shotgun, and shot Raymond in the stomach. He was rushed to Morningside Hospital, but died while undergoing surgery.

The Investigation:
Nothing of substance was investigated.

Suspects:

Police never made any arrests for Raymond Washington's murder. Rumors say that members of the Hoover Crips (now the Hoover Criminals) were responsible, but this was never proven. A rash of shootings then started between Raymond's Eastside Crips (now known as the East Coast Crips) and the Hoover Crips.

Current Status of Case:
At the same time as the war between the Eastside Crips and Hoover Crips, a fight erupted over a woman between the Eight Trey Gangster Crips and Rollin' 60's Crips. Shootings also took place between those gangs, both large and very violent factions of the Crips. Other Crips chose a side, and Crips members have been killing fellow members ever since. More die at their own members' hands than by any other gang. One can't help but think that Raymond would have been very disappointed by where the gang he founded ended up.

Victim: Christine Jessop
Date: October 3, 1984
Location: A convenience store near her home in Queensville, Ontario
Suspect: Guy Paul Morin

Backstory:
Christine Jessop was a 9 year-old girl from Queensville, Ontario. She was born to Janet and Bob Jessop on November 29, 1974. She was a bit of a tomboy and loved sports, especially baseball. She also had a sensitive side and was a kind girl. She had an older brother, Kenneth.

Christine was in the fourth grade at Queensville Public School, and was 4ft 9in tall. She weighed only about 40 pounds soaking wet, her family joked. Her mother would later report to the police that she had no reason to run away.

On The Day in Question:
October 3, 1984 was like any other day. At 3:50pm Christine alighted from the school bus and entered her home, picking up the mail on her way. She was home alone, as her mom and brother were finishing errands. Her dad was in jail at the time so was not at home.

We know that somewhere between 4:00-4:30pm she went to a convenience store near to her house, where she purchased bubble gum. That was the last time anyone saw Christine alive.

Her mom and brother arrived home at 4:10pm, and seeing her bag on the counter along with a newspaper and mail, looked for Christine. When they couldn't find her, they called her friends, and began to search the neighborhood, including a park nearby. No one reported seeing her.

Somewhere between 7:00-8:00pm, her mother, called the police.

The Investigation:
Within just minutes of Janet's phone call, police were searching the area. They also interviewed the Jessop's neighbors, and their attention soon turned to their immediate next-door neighbor, a man by the name of Guy Paul Morin. Aged twenty-three, other neighbors said to police that he was 'weird'.

During a search, a police dog indicated towards Morin's car. A subsequent search inside the car revealed fibers, which the Ontario police forensic team reported were from Christine.

It wasn't until December 31, 1985 that Christine's body was discovered, in a field nearby to Sunderland, over 30 miles from her home.

She was unnaturally posed, lying on her back with her legs spread. She wore both a pullover and turtleneck sweater, and a blouse with buttons that were missing, along with two pairs of socks. Her panties were found near her right foot. Found just south of her body were corduroy pants, including a belt, and a pair of Nike shoes.

An autopsy revealed she had been stabbed to death, with multiple blows inflicted. Semen was also found, but DNA testing in criminal cases did not yet exist.

Suspects:
Guy Paul Morin was a suspect from early in the case. He lived with his parents, and worked at a local furniture store. He also played both saxophone and clarinet in a band. He kept bees as a hobby, another 'oddity' according to the neighbors.

Morin had little contact with his peers, and didn't go out to bars or other similar venues. Instead, he spent most of his time on his hobbies. However, he did have a girlfriend, and had never before been in any trouble with the police.

When he was interviewed, detectives would later testify that they found his actions 'strange', and that he would stare straight ahead and never speak during the interviews.

After multiple interviews with police, Morin was arrested and charged with Christine's rape and murder. He went to trial in January 1986.

The Trial:
The prosecution's theory in Morin's trial was that he was an already odd man who had simply snapped on the day in question. He raped, and then murdered Christine, and then disposed of her body miles away in the field.

During the trial, technicians reported that the red fibers they had found in his car had come from the sweater Christine had been wearing. Two jailhouse snitches (one of whom has not been identified) testified that Morin had confessed to them, while he was in jail awaiting trial.

Despite this, Morin was acquitted on February 7, 1986, due to little evidence. In Canada, the prosecution is allowed to appeal for a new trial if the suspect is acquitted, which they did and won the right to another trial in 1987.

Morin's second trial was delayed until 1992 due to his own appeals based on the failure of the Crown to disclose exculpatory evidence, among other things.

In the second trial, the same evidence was presented, but this time the snitches were viewed in a more favorable light by the jury. Forensic technicians again testified on the fibers, and also that just one hair on a necklace worn by Christine matched Morin's. On July 23, 1992 he was found guilty of first-degree murder, and sentenced to life in prison.

Classed as a child killer in prison, he was abused and also raped by other inmates, all while his attorney worked to appeal for a third trial. While this appeal was still pending, DNA science progressed to the point it could test the DNA found on Christine's body. It did not match Morin.

On January 23, 1995 his appeal was granted, and thanks to the DNA report his conviction was set aside. A directed verdict (one made when the judge decides the jury couldn't possibly reach any other decision) of a full acquittal was entered.

After his release, Morin was awarded nearly $1.5M in compensation. Also, an inquest conducted to discover how his trial went so wrong shown a hard light on the Canadian justice system. It found that the prosecution had withheld from the defense exculpatory evidence, which is evidence that is favorable to the defendant, and usually tends to prove them innocent. Technicians in the lab had also contaminated the samples, but had withheld that fact from the defense. The two snitches had been coached by police, and also received a sentence reduction themselves in return for their testimony.

The inquest found that the police had focused in on Morin from the beginning, despite the fact that he had an airtight alibi. Some reports say that the police even did such things as convince Christine's mother to say they had arrived home at 4:35pm instead of 4:10pm, as Morin couldn't have been home earlier than 4:15pm. The Jessops later apologized to Morin.

Current Status of Case:
Christine's murderer is still unknown.

Murder in the Mist - Dian Fossey

Victim: Dian Fossey
Date: December 26, 1985
Location: Her cabin in the research camp, the
Virunga Mountains, Rwanda, Africa
Suspects: Emmanuel Rwelekana, Wayne McGuire,
Protais Zigiranyirazo (known as Mr. Z)

Backstory:
Dian Fossey was born in 1932, in San Francisco. Her
parents divorced when she was six years old, and she
was raised by her mother, Kitty, along with her
stepfather, whom her mother married one year after
her divorce. Dian's stepfather was very strict, to the
point of not even allowing her to sit with him and her
mother for family meals at the dining table. Her father
tried to stay in contact with her, but her mother
discouraged it, and eventually all contact was lost.
Her father eventually committed suicide when he was
fifty.

Dian left home to go to college, and after that only
ever returned for brief visits. At first she enrolled in
business school, on the advice of her stepfather.
However, she enrolled in a course studying pre-
veterinary science at the University of California at the
age of 19. But, Dian then decided to switch majors
and transferred to San Jose State College to study
occupational therapy. In 1954, she graduated and
started working with autistic children in Louisville,
Kentucky.

A tall young woman, at just under 6ft tall, and with
beautiful auburn hair, Dian had grown into a strikingly
beautiful woman. After she graduated, in part through

the influence of two close friends, Dian became obsessed with the idea of going on safari to Africa. The trip cost as much as a whole year's wage, and so when she couldn't afford to go, one of these friends proposed and offered the safari trip as a honeymoon. However, Dian turned him down.

Instead, she saved as much as she could for two years, and then took out a loan against her future income to cover the rest. On September 26, 1963, she was on her way. Dian was going to visit Zaire, Kenya, Rwanda, Rhodesia, Tanganyika (now Tanzania) and Uganda. While on her travels she took hundreds of photos, and many reels of 9mm film, as well as kept a journal every night. She was aiming to write about her travels when she got home, and submit them for publication.

During the second week of her trip, Dian met someone who would change her life – she met Louis Leakey. Louis, the son of two British missionaries, was now a famous archeologist. At the time, she had no idea how important he would become in her life.

Also on the trip, she was allowed to tag along with two wildlife filmmakers, Alan and Joan Root. It was with them that she first saw the mountain gorillas, and knew immediately that she'd be back.

On her return to the United States, she tried to sell her photos and articles, but she met with little success. Three years later, she attended a lecture tour that Leakey was presenting. He recognized her, and she told him of her dream to work with gorillas. Fate must have been smiling on Dian, as it was at that same moment that Louis was interviewing for a position for a long-term study of the gorillas. He had other candidates with more scientific experience, but from his own experiences with Jane Goodall, he thought a mature woman would be better suited for the role. Three weeks later, Dian was offered the job. Originally starting in the Congo, she moved the research to Rwanda in 1967, after being removed from the original camp by Congo soldiers, for their own safety. It was here in Rwanda that she first founded the Karisoke Research Centre.

Dian was very successful in her early work. In 1970, National Geographic published images of her communicating with the gorillas, and these captured the hearts of everyone who saw them. However, she did not get along so well with her employees, and never had anything good to say about them in her journals and letters. She also disliked the natives, who allowed their animals to graze in the national park. The group she hated most, however, was the poachers.

Dian lobbied the Rwandan government to setup anti-poaching patrols, and she would even attack them herself, pretending to perform 'black magic' to scare them. She held their cattle for ransom, and set their camps on fire. She had an ongoing dispute with one particular poacher, Munyarukikio, and she even kidnapped his child for a day, before returning him. After her favourite gorilla was killed, and the evidence pointed to Munyarukiko, she abandoned her research work and instead turned 'active conservationist'. She posted photos of the dead and mutilated gorilla about the place, and told her students to carry guns.

A villager admitted that Munyarukiki's clan was responsible for the gorilla's death, and she held the villager hostage for several days. This act earned her an official warning from both National Geographic and the Rwandan government. She dismissed a warning from a Belgian Colonial Governor, who also warned her regarding her actions. Later events would prove that she should have listened.

As time went by, Dian became more and more obsessed with 'saving' the gorillas, and grew reportedly more and more 'strange'. She was often drunk, and other staff members tried to take over leadership of the research center. People begin to think that poachers were killing the gorillas as a personal vendetta toward Dian. Finally, in 1979, she was told by National Geographic and the Leakey Foundation that they would pull funding for the center, unless she took extended leave. In March 1980, Dian finally left, after a long fight. She spent most of the next three years in the USA.

During this time, Dian published the extremely popular book *Gorillas in the Mist*, and in 1983, returned to Rwanda. However, Dian now started to question whether the huge amount of tourists her own work attracted was now doing more harm to the gorillas than the poachers ever did. She started to give public interviews regarding this, threatening a large revenue stream for an otherwise very poor country.

On The Night in Question:
During the fall of 1985, events started occurring that foreshadowed Dian's eventual demise. Firstly, her pet parrot died, apparently poisoned. A couple of days

later, she found a puff adder carved of wood on her front doorstep. According to local customs, this said she was marked for death.

Two months after this, on December 26, a person or persons broke into her cabin while she was sleeping, cutting a hole in the wall. Dian apparently woke up, as her gun and ammunition clip were in her hand. She was killed by two strikes from a bush machete, before she could get off a shot.

Dian's body was found by an African aid at sunrise. The floor was covered in broken glass, a table in the room was overturned, and the mattress was sitting on an odd angle. It's believed that Dian went to her death fighting. All of Dian's valuables were still in the cabin, including her passport, and thousands of dollars worth of traveler's checks and US currency. Therefore, robbery was ruled out as a motive.

In the days immediately following her death, even her colleagues were less than gracious on hearing the news of her death, and were openly critical of her behavior.

Dian left all her belongings, including any proceeds from *Gorillas in the Mist* to her anti-poaching fund. However, her mother challenged the will in court and won.

Suspects:
At first, after her death, Dian's entire staff was arrested. All were later released, except one, an African native. Emmanuel Rwelekana, a native African guide that Dian had fired, was detained by the police.

The Investigation:
Rwandan 'kangaroo courts' quickly convicted two men, the man they detained and an American staff member Wayne McGuire, after intense pressure from the media coverage of her life and death. However, most international authorities believe that these two men were merely government scapegoats.

Arrangements had been made out of public view before McGuire was charged that meant McGuire could return home. He was convicted in absentia by the Rwandan court. Because no extradition treaty exists between Rwanda and the US, McGuire has not served any of his sentence and most believe him totally innocent.

The second man, Rwelekana, reportedly hanged himself in prison before he could be tried, after being held in prison for nine months.

In 1988, the movie *Gorillas in the Mist* was released, and this reignited interest in Dian's case. This time, a new suspect came to light, one with high connections in the government. Informants reported that the murder of Dian Fossey had been ordered by Protais Zigiranyirazo, known as Mr. Z. He was the brother in law of the then president of Rwanda, and prefect of the Ruhengeri province, where Dian's research center and the gorilla's habitat were located.

Like many officials, Mr. Z had a number of businesses on the side, on top of his official duties. These made him very rich, while the majority of the country lived in poverty. International authorities believe it was his financial interests in gorilla tourism that lead him to order Dian's death. However, events that stunned the world would delay any investigation.

In April 1994, the president of Rwanda was killed in an airplane crash. The crash was viewed as an assassination. Both the president and Mr. Z were Hutus, who were the majority ethnicity in Rwanda. In revenge for the president's death, his widow, Mr. Z, the military, and other government officials planned a campaign of genocide of the Tutsi minority. Hundreds of thousands of Tutsi citizens were killed over four months.

Eventually, after four years in hiding, Mr. Z was arrested in 2001 in Belgium, for his part in the Rwandan Genocide.

The Trial:
In 2001, Mr. Z was charged with two counts of crimes against humanity by the International Criminal Tribunal of Rwanda. Pending his second appearance on November 25, 2003, the indictment was amended to add accusations of committing genocide against the Tutsi's.

On December 18, 2008, Mr. Z was convicted and sentenced to twenty years imprisonment, plus fifteen years to be served concurrently for aiding and abetting genocide. However, this was overturned on an appeal on November 16, 2009. His immediate release was ordered. Some say he was released on a technicality.

Mr. Z is now publicly acknowledged by Rwanda as the head of Dian Fossey's murder plot, but because of the magnitude of the Rwandan Genocide, it's unlikely he will ever be formally charged with her murder.

Current Status of Case:
On December 31, 1985, Fossey was buried with her beloved gorillas. At first her grave was marked with a simple wooden cross in the same style Dian herself used for the gorillas. Later, a more permanent headstone was installed.

Ape tourism has resumed in Rwanda, and the country has also embraced gorillas as their national symbol. Rwanda charges $250 per tourist to view them, which is just about the same as the national per-capita annual income of the country's residents. The money motivated the government to finally get tough on poaching, and it is much less prevalent today.

There are now estimated to be 350 mountain gorillas in the area, 100 more than Fossey's original estimates from 1968. A conservation fund she created is now named after her. The fund continues her protection of the gorillas and sponsors safari visits to the same jungle where she once played with her apes.

A Lasting Legacy - Amber Hagerman, AMBER Alert

Victim: Amber Rene Hagerman
Date: January 17, 1996
Location: An abandoned parking lot, Arlington, Texas
Suspect: None

Backstory:
Amber Rene Hagerman was a nine year old from Arlington, Texas. She had a five year-old brother, Ricky. Amber was born November 25, 1986 to Richard Hagerman and Donna Whitson. At the time of the incident, Donna and Amber were included in a local TV show's research on families that were struggling to get off welfare.

Her grandparents have said that Amber was a beautiful child, who loved to cook with grandma and play tea parties with her little brother. She was out of her mother's sight for only minutes when the incident occurred.

On The Day in Question:
Amber Hagerman was abducted while visiting her grandparents in Arlington, Texas. Amber was visiting with her mother, Donna, and her five year old brother Ricky. They arrived at their grandparent's house around 3pm on Saturday January 13, 1996.

The grandparents kept two bicycles at their house for the children, and Amber and Ricky asked if they could go for a ride. Jimmie, the children's grandfather, and Donna told them yes, but to just go once around the block.

Jimmie was working on a car in the front yard. He called out a greeting to Amber as they went past.

Two corners away, in the abandoned parking lot of a Winn-Dixie store that had been shut down, neighborhood kids had set up a ramp. The spot was busy, and it was the middle of the day and broad daylight. The children stopped for a few minutes at the ramp.

Ricky soon appeared back home, and when he was asked where Amber was, said that she'd stayed behind to have one more go on the ramp. He was sent back to retrieve her, but came back a few minutes later, saying he couldn't find her.

Jimmie jumped in his truck, and sped to the parking lot, where he found a police car already there. The officer told Jimmie that a man who lived nearby had reported hearing screaming and seeing a man carry off a young girl into a pickup truck. The man had called 911, but when police arrived the only thing they'd found at the scene was a bicycle. It was Amber's.

It had only been eight minutes since her mom and grandparents had waved Amber off to ride around the block.

The Investigation:
Amber's case attracted a large media following, and her mom also appeared on TV, pleading for her release.

The sole witness, Jim Kevil, was also interviewed. He described the man as either white or Hispanic, with a dark truck, but said it all happened too fast for any other detail.

Police believe that Amber was taken by someone who was a stranger to her. The vast majority of children reported missing in the United States are runaways or abducted by family members. Only about 100 reports each year are of stranger abductions. However, strikingly, out of these cases, 9 out of 10 victims are female, half are sexually assaulted and in the end 3 out of 4 are killed within 3 hours of the abduction.

The truck described by the witness had also been seen outside a Laundromat near the parking lot before Amber was snatched. The police theorized that her abduction was a crime of opportunity.

The police formed a taskforce with the FBI. Amber's case was so well known with the media that she became known as Arlington's Child.

No other witness was ever found, and no demands or contact were ever made from the kidnapper.

Four days later, a man walking his dog along a creek bed found her naked body lying in the creek bed, near an apartment complex in North Arlington. She had been brutally murdered, her throat slit.

The Suspect:
Three weeks after Amber's abduction, the authorities released a profile of the killer. They suggested he was male, and at least 25 years old. He lived or worked near the spot her body was dumped. Something had happened, it was theorized, to make the killer snap, and his personality or appearance may have since been changed due to this trauma.

Police believed that because he held Amber for two days before killing her, there must be a crime scene full of physical evidence somewhere, but it was never found.

Following the release of the profile, police followed up 5,500 leads over 18 months, but nothing ever led to the killer. After spending more than $1 million, the taskforce was disbanded in the summer of 1997.

Current Status of Case:
Amber's abduction and death, while tragic, also left a huge legacy. After her murder, a man from Dallas asked why, in cases such as this where every minute matters, can't police and media collaborate to urgently release the information to the public, such as they do with weather warnings.

Television and radio took on the idea, and in July 1997, the Dallas Amber Plan was put into action. The plan proved its value sixteen months later. Sandra Fallis, a babysitter who had problems with drugs, took an eight week-old baby with her and disappeared. An alert went out and she was found within ninety minutes. A driver heard the alert and spotted her truck. The child was returned safely.

In 2000, Houston setup its own Amber Plan. In 2002 Texas set it up statewide. The U.S. Justice Department started to co-ordinate the program for states and cities in 2002. Today, all states and many individual cities have Amber Alert Plans. The Federal government estimates that 240 children have been found because of the alerts. In 1999, eight children were recovered, and in 2003, seventy-two were.

While the system has its share of criticisms, Amber's family is proud of their daughter and granddaughter's legacy. Arlington officials have planted a tree near the scene of her abduction in her memory. The fence surrounding it is decorated in pink ribbons.

Amber's abduction and murder remains unsolved.

The Ignored Victims - Evelyn Hernandez, and children

Victims: Evelyn Hernandez, Alex Hernandez, unborn baby boy Hernandez
Date: May 1, 2002
Location: The Crocker-Amazon neighborhood, San Francisco, California
Suspect: Herman Aguilera

Backstory:
Evelyn Hernandez was a twenty-four year old woman from San Francisco. She was an immigrant from El Salvador, and a single mother. At the time of her disappearance, she had a five year old son, and was just weeks away from delivering her second son.

Evelyn came to the United States when she was fourteen years old, and joined her mother, Maria Luisa. Maria had fled El Salvador due to civil war.

Evelyn enrolled in school, and also took extra English classes. Workers at a Latino youth center she attended mentioned she was shy, but intelligent, and described her as hard working.

Growing up, Evelyn developed a strong interest in acting, and performed in many plays at the youth center. Her son, Alex, was born out of wedlock, but Evelyn still finished school.

After graduation, she held many different jobs to support her son, including a nurse's aide, store clerk and waitress. Friends described her as lonely.

Evelyn met Herman Aguilera, a mechanic at San Francisco International Airport, and they started dating. Towards the end of 2001, when she was expecting a child with him, she discovered that he was already married. She allegedly told him that she didn't want to see him again. It was shortly after that she disappeared.

On The Day in Question:
Evelyn, along with her five year-old son, disappeared on May 1, 2002. Two months later, on July 24, a torso was found floating in the bay, near the city's landmark Bay Bridge. DNA evidence confirmed it belonged to Evelyn Hernandez. The rest of her remains, and any from her son, have never been found.

The Investigation:
At first, police thought that Evelyn may have simply gone away somewhere else to have her baby, and didn't hold a news conference for more than a month after her disappearance. Despite this, police had admitted that it is extremely rare for a woman to disappear when pregnant, and when they do the number one cause is murder.

A day or two after she initially went missing, a wallet with two $20 bills and a check made out to Evelyn was found in the street. Her boyfriend, Herman Aguilera, had originally reported her missing, but police attention shifted to him as a suspect when it was revealed that Evelyn's wallet was found just down the block from a gas station that the limousine company Aguilera worked at used regularly.

Evelyn's relatives reported that there had been an argument between the couple, and that Aguilera was extremely angry towards her. They alleged that he didn't want to keep the baby, and he didn't want to pay her any child support.

The police reported that Evelyn had been growing concerned as to how she would support a second child, and had told Aguilera she was considering legal action to ensure the child was supported.

The Suspect:
Evelyn's boyfriend, Herman Aguilera, was questioned by the police, but was never arrested or even formally named as a suspect. His wife provided him with an alibi for the night Evelyn disappeared, however she did not know at that time that Evelyn had been pregnant by her husband.

Current Status of Case:
A year after her disappearance, the mayor's office listed a $10,000 reward.

Years after she disappeared, the case has now attracted some media attention. Parallels have been drawn between this and another case, that of Laci Peterson, a 27 year old from Modesto, California, who went missing when pregnant, on Christmas Eve, 2002. Laci's husband was arrested and convicted of the crime.

Friends and family of Evelyn Hernandez have accused law enforcement and the media of not caring about Evelyn's case simply because she wasn't white. The Laci Peterson case garnered far more attention in the media. The lawyer for Scott Peterson (Laci's husband) has even suggested that her murder was committed by the same person who killed Evelyn, but the police do not agree.

Evelyn, her son Alex and her unborn son's murders remains unsolved.

A Family Destroyed: The Seewen Murder Case

Victims: Eugen Siegrist-Säckinger, Elsa Siegrist-Säckinger, Anna Westhäuser-Siegrist, Emanual Westhäuser, Max Westhäuser
Date: Pentecost Weekend, 1976
Location: Seewen, Switzerland
Suspects: Carl Doser, Adolf 'Johnny' Siegrist

The Seewen murders were the biggest crime in the history of Switzerland. It remains today the biggest mass murder case in the country's history.

In total, five people were murdered. They were husband and wife Eugen Siegrist-Säckinger (63) and Elsa Clara Siegrist-Säckinger (62), Eugen's sister Anna Westhäuser-Siegrist (80), and Anna's two sons, Emanuel Westhäuser (52) and Max Westhäuser (49).

On The Day in Question:
No one knows exactly when the murders took place, but it is known to have occurred sometime over Pentecost Weekend in 1976, which that year fell on June 6. The family was spending time at their weekend house, which was located, along with a small garden, in the forest in Seewen, a municipality in Switzerland.

All of the victims were killed with a total of thirteen rounds, shot from a Winchester rifle. A woman walking nearby discovered the bodies on June 6th. The police found four bodies inside the house. The fifth was rolled up in a carpet and placed on the terrace.

The Investigation:

The murders were immediately notable due to the precision and almost execution style, of the shots. Every shot was perfectly placed, with one victim shot in the head four times.

Investigators followed all leads, and searched for all the owners of Winchester rifles, which had been determined to be the murder weapon, but nothing was ever found.

Police believe that the original targets of the shooting were Elsa and Eugen, and the killer was merely surprised by the presence of the others.

Suspects:
Little hope was given to ever solving the case. Then, 20 years after the murders, in 1996, a Winchester rifle was found hidden in the walls of a house that belonged to a woman with the surname Doser. The gun was identified as belonging to a man named Carl Doser, and was an imitation Italian Winchester rifle, with a short barrel. Tests revealed that it was the murder weapon.

Doser was a bit of a loner who lived in Basel, about 14 miles away from Seewen. He had purchased the gun from Hofmann & Reinhart Waffen AG in 1973. Doser had originally been interviewed by police regarding his gun, but had lied and said that he sold it at a flea market.
However, police never found a motive for Doser to murder the family, and they could not prove that Doser had ever met the victims. He was never charged, but to this day most people in Switzerland think he was guilty.

An alternative suspect was Adolf 'Johnny' Siegrist. Siegrist was related to the family, and was reported to the police by a colleague Hans Blaser, who thought he was the guilty party.

Blaser was a combat shooter, and reported that Siegrist had asked him for a machine pistol. Siegrist was only around 4' 11" tall and had a higher than normal voice, which reportedly gave him an inferiority complex. Eugen and Elsa Siegrist-Säckinger, the two victims who police suspected were the targets, had given him the nicknames of Dölfeli, a demeaning name for Adolf and Globi, the name of a character in a popular children's book.

It's also possible that Siegrist was the one who purchased the bullets for the Winchester rifle. A shop assistant remembers a customer buying two packages of .38 Special ammunition. He asked for those with an extra heavy lead bullet, and then asked if the rounds would fit a Winchester rifle. He mentioned he was buying it for somebody else, and used an insulting Italian phrase to describe the gun.

Those who knew him described Adolf as quick to anger. When police searched his flat, they found Styrofoam model heads. Each had been shot. He was arrested briefly, but died in the mid 1980's, having never been found guilty.

Trial:
Due to lack of evidence, Doser and Siegrist were never charged and there was no trial.

Current Status of Case:
Unsolved

A Holy Murder: Óscar Romero, Archbishop of San Salvador

Victims: Óscar Arnulfo Romero y Galdámez
Date: March 24, 1980
Location: La Divina Providencia chapel, San Miguel, El Salvador
Suspects: Roberto D'Aubuisson, Oscar Perez Linares, Alvaro Saravia

Backstory:
Óscar Arnulfo Romero y Galdámez was a bishop of the Catholic Church in the country of El Salvador, and became the fourth Archbishop of the city of San Salvador.

Born on August 15th, 1917, Romero came from a large family. He had five brothers, and two sisters, one of which died shortly after birth. At the age of one, he was baptized into the Catholic Church. He spent much of his free time at the town's churches when he was growing up.

Romero grew up during a difficult time for the Church in his home country. The Church was, at the time, being persecuted, and many people were being assassinated or killed. Thirteen wealthy families owned 40% of the land in El Salvador.

When Romero was thirteen years told, he entered the minor seminary. He was promoted to the national seminary in San Salvador, and graduated from the Gregorian University in Rome, as a Licentiate in Theology. On April 4th, 1942, he was ordained in Rome. Unfortunately due to travel restrictions brought on by World War II, his family was unable to attend.

Romero continued to study in Italy, and was working toward a doctoral degree in theology. In 1943 at the age of twenty-six he was called back home by the Bishop. On his way home, he was detained by the Cuban police for having travelled from 'Fascist Italy' (a term that applied from 1922 to 1943, when Mussolini was in power), and was placed in an internment camp.

After several months in prison, his travelling companion, Father Valladares, became sick, and with help from other priests, they were transferred to a hospital. From there, they were released from Cuba and allowed to continue home.

Romero first worked as a parish priest, but then moved to San Miguel, El Salvador where he worked for more than twenty years. It was here that he supported many groups, including starting an Alcoholics Anonymous group.

Archbishop Romero was very vocal in his opposition to poverty and human injustices.

On The Day in Question:
On March 24, 1980, Romero was celebrating Mass at a small chapel named *La Divina Providencia*. Only one day before, he had delivered a sermon where he called on Salvadoran soldiers to cease carrying out what he called government repression, and violations of basic human rights. As he finished his sermon and was moving back to the middle of the altar, a shot rang out, killing him.

His funeral was held on March 30, and was attended by more than 250,000 people, from all over the world. Some viewed the massive attendance as a protest against the government.

During the ceremony, smoke bombs exploded in nearby streets, and gunfire came from buildings surrounding the cathedral where the funeral was held. Many people were killed, both from the gunfire directly and the stampeding crowd running away from the explosions and bullets. The official figure is 31 dead, but journalists' reports place it more likely somewhere between 30-50 people.

Some have accused the government of being the ones who set the bombs and fired the shots, but the real truth will likely never be known.

The Investigation:
The USA had been heavily involved in funding the rebels acting against the El Salvadoran government. When Romero was assassinated, President Reagan vowed to make the capture and punishment of Romero's killers a priority.

In the end, the investigation came up with nothing. No one was able to identify anyone who pulled the trigger. No witnesses came forward. The official line was that there was a lack of evidence to arrest or convict anyone.

Suspects:
Roberto D'Aubuisson was a military intelligence officer who had recently left the army. In the weeks leading up to the murder, he had repeatedly been on television using military intelligence to denounce

'guerrillas'. Those that D'Aubisson accused were often murdered, and this time, Romero was at the top of his list.

The security chief for D'Aubuisson, Álvaro Rafael Saravia, has often been named as the person who actually pulled the trigger. The Center For Justice and Accountability, a United States human rights organization, found Saravia liable for being involved in the assassination and ordered that he pay $10M for 'crimes against humanity'. None of the money has ever been paid.

Trial:
D'Aubuisson was the number one suspect but was never charged and no trial was held.

Current Status of Case:
In 1997, Pope John Paul II bestowed upon Romero the title of Servant of God. This is a title used by multiple religions, generally used to describe someone who is pious in their faith. In the Catholic Church in particular, it also signifies that the person is being investigated for potential sainthood. Many consider Romero an unofficial patron saint of El Salvador. The canonization procedure is still underway.

Roberto D'Aubuisson went on to become one of El Salvador's most successful politicians. He died of cancer on February 20th, 1992 near the end of the civil war.

Conspiracy theories still abound, suggesting that the US Government knew much more than it let on, but did nothing in fear of jeopardizing the war effort. Key witnesses, including the most likely assassin, were in turn killed by those who were supposed to be investigating Romero's death.

Declassified CIA files have since named Oscar Perez Linares, a national police detective, as the killer. This has been supported by accounts told to journalists and accounts from other Salvadoran officials. Linares himself has since been killed when he was captured trying to flee to Guatemala, escaping from a special police unit that the USA helped setup to investigate crimes against human rights. The truth about the Archbishop's death has likely gone to the grave with him.

A Mr. Cruel Murder: Karmein Chan

Victims: Karmein Chan
Date: April 12, 1991
Location: The Chan home in Templestowe near Melbourne, Australia
Suspect: 'Mr. Cruel'

Backstory:
Karmein Chan was born on November 5th, 1977 to John and Phyllis Chan, a Chinese couple who owned three Chinese restaurants in Eltham, near Melbourne Australia. Karmein also had two younger sisters. The Chans' hard work and long hours had paid off and the family lived in the well-to-do area of Templestowe in a luxurious home. Karmein frequently watched her younger sisters while their parents attended to the family businesses.

On the Night in Question:
On Saturday, April 13th, 1991, the then thirteen year-old Karmein Chan was abducted from her home. The three sisters were forced into a back bedroom by a masked stranger who had gained entry into their home. The two younger girls were then locked in a closet and a bed was placed against the closet door. The girls were eventually able to free themselves and contact their parents. The man and their sister were gone.

A car in the home's front yard was spray painted with the words 'Pay Up Asian Drug Dealer, More and More to Come'. However, police believe this was left to distract from the killer's real motive, rather than being the true motivations of the abductor.

The case attracted huge media attention, with Chan's distraught parents being featured on news broadcasts. Unfortunately, some now believe that the search and investigation may have been hampered by the release of an old school photo of Chan being used in the reports. The photo did not accurately represent how she appeared at the time of her abduction.

Knowing that the man police suspected had eventually released his other victims, Chan's parents hoped that their daughter would soon be home. However, time passed and there was no sign of Chan or contact from her abductor.

A year later, her badly decomposed body was found on the northern outskirts of Melbourne. On April 9th, 1992, a man walking his dog along a creek in a northern Melbourne suburb found what looked like a human skull sitting in a landfill area. The area had recently been worked over by bulldozers. He went home and called police.

The Investigation:
The Chan abduction inflamed an already hot story, with at least two other cases involving abductions of young girls in the same area since 1988. The crimes were all of a similar nature and the suspect soon began to be called 'Mr. Cruel'. A poster was created showing photographs of the three victims, and offered a reward of $300,000 for information leading to the arrest of the suspected perpetrator. This reward is still available today.

In an unprecedented move, every single home in the state of Victoria, Australia received a copy of the poster, along with some homes in other states. Massive versions were posted on billboards and hundreds were displayed on public transport.

The area where the skull was found was sealed off, and police painstakingly searched and eventually exhumed the badly decomposed human remains. DNA and dental records confirmed it was Chan's body. Examination of the remains revealed that she had been shot in the back of the head at least three times.

Four weeks after Chan's abduction, a taskforce was started. Called Operation Spectrum, it consisted of 40 police, and spent almost three years, and $3.8 million trying to solve the crime and capture Mr. Cruel. It remains the biggest operation in Victorian Police history, and involved investigations right across the country. Police even interviewed people from Britain and the United States.

Both of Mr. Cruel's previous victims reported aspects of a house they were held in, and commented they could hear planes flying overhead. Police examined flight plans in detail, but after spending months searching homes across fifteen suburbs, a house that matches the girls' descriptions has never been found.

Critics of Chan's case have reported that the crime scene was not properly secured, and people were 'stomping all over the place'. This has gone on to influence how other crimes are investigated in the future and was the catalyst for new official guidelines to be created for the police force.

On December 14th, 2010, the Victorian Police announced they had established a taskforce eight months earlier, and had been following new evidence. Chan's case remains unsolved.

Suspect:
Although he has never been formally identified, most believe Chan's abduction and murder to be committed by a man named aptly by the police as Mr. Cruel. He has never been identified, let alone charged with any offence. Police believe he is responsible for a string of rapes and murders of girls across the 1980's and early 1990's in Melbourne, Australia.

Current Status of Case:
The failure to secure the crime scene in Chan's case was not the first time that evidence was lost from a crime scene suspected to be the work of the same perpetrator. Police suspect that Mr. Cruel was almost certainly involved in a series of attacks across Melbourne in the early to mid 1980's. Of particular disappointment was the disappearance of tape that had been used to bind one of his victims. Since the 1980's, great strides have been made in forensic technologies, and many believe that sampling of the smallest pieces of evidence would now be possible. He was not as careful with his earlier victims as he was with later cases, and may well have left DNA evidence behind.

The taskforce setup to investigate these cases changed the way that all detectives conduct investigations, and new minimum standards for major crime investigations have been introduced.

Although the taskforce didn't catch Mr. Cruel, it did still achieve something worthwhile. From the investigations, over seventy people were charged with offenses including rape, blackmail, incest, and possession of child pornography. Legislation was also strengthened regarding sex offenders and their access to areas frequented by children.

The Lady in the Trunk: Anne Barber Dunlap

Victims: Ann Barber Dunlap
Date: New Years Weekend 1995
Location: Kmart Parking Lot in Minneapolis, Minnesota
Suspect: Brad Dunlap

Backstory:
Anne Dunlap was 31 years old when she disappeared. A Pillsbury marketing executive, she was married and lived in Minnesota. Anne was living with her husband at her parent's house near Lake Calhoun in Minneapolis, while the couple built a new home.

On the Day in Question:
Anne disappeared over New Year's weekend in 1995. On December 30th, 1995, Dunlap had lunch with friends. Her husband reported that she had plans to go to the Mall of America to go shoe shopping. In interviews, he has stated that she was supposed to meet him around 4:30pm to run an errand together, and then go out for dinner. His story is that Anne never arrived, and he then reported her missing.

Police were unable to verify whether Anne ever went to the mall. However a private investigator hired by Brad Dunlap claims to have at least two witnesses that saw Anne at the mall on December 30th, 1995.

The next day, friends found her car in the parking lot of Kmart, just a few miles from Dunlap's parent's house. Police soon arrived, along with a bloodhound. They combed the area for clues. Family and friends of Anne were already thinking the worst.

When police opened the trunk of the car, they found Anne's body inside. She had been stabbed repeatedly in the throat and neck. Police reports stated that a lot of blood was found in the trunk. Reports from the media also indicated that Anne was not sexually assaulted. A diamond ring she had been wearing had been stolen.

The Investigation:
Early suspicion fell to Dunlap's husband, Brad. Police discovered that just a few months before the murder, he had purchased a $1 million life insurance policy on her.

Brad Dunlap was interviewed by police, over a five hour period. He claimed that he had been running errands before he was supposed to meet Anne, but the store owner of a shop he claimed to have visited disagreed with Brad's claim. Brad stated that the store in question had been closed when he tried to visit, but the store owner went on record saying that he had been open at that time, and that Brad never visited his store without his wife. Other evidence has also called his alibi into question, such as security camera footage from another store, but it remains inconclusive.

Police searched Anne's parent's home repeatedly for evidence. Over the following months, Brad continued to live there with them.

Suspect:
Police were quick to suspect Anne's husband, Brad Dunlap, and he remains a focus of police attention.

He has never been arrested for the crime, and to this day insists he is innocent.

Current Status of the Case:
Dunlap's parents, Donn and Louise Barber, have helped ten women to attend school with a scholarship for MBA candidates, created in her memory, at Dunlap's alma mater.

Brad Dunlap has remarried and moved to Arizona. He still keeps in touch with Dunlap's parents, and they visit him every year. They believe Brad is innocent.

Brad Dunlap sued Chubb Insurance Co. of America when they refused to pay Anne's life insurance policy. The insurance company claimed that through documents obtained from the Minneapolis Police, they determined Brad intended to murder Anne when he took out the policy. On September 30th, 1997 a U.S. District Court judge ruled that police had to therefore turn over all documents to Dunlap's lawyers, and that they also be allowed to examine all physical evidence in the case. He ruled that confidentiality was no longer a question because the police themselves had shared the material with a third party. Brad claimed he increased the amount of the policy due to the value of the new house they were building together. In 1998, Chubb Insurance settled for an undisclosed amount.

An Anne Barber Dunlap Memorial Walk was opened at the Minnesota Landscape Arboretum in July 1998.

A Pocketful of Clues: Ricky McCormick

Victims: Ricky McCormick
Date: June 26, 1999
Location: A cornfield in St. Charles County near St. Louis, Missouri
Suspect/s: Gregory Lamar Knox, Baha Hamdallah

Backstory:
Ricky McCormick was 41 years old and lived in St Louis, Missouri. He stood out from his peers as being a little 'different'. When he was growing up, his mother called him 'retarded'. He was extremely close to his cousin, Charles McCormick. Charles reported that Ricky often talked like he was from another world. He suspects Ricky may have been schizophrenic or suffered from bipolar disorder.

Reports are unclear as to whether Ricky was ever treated for mental illness, but family members recall many occasions where his tall tales and unusual behavior would get him into trouble. He was always passed to the next grade in school. Despite this, when he dropped out of school, he was illiterate.

Ricky survived on odd jobs such as mopping floors, washing dishes and service station attendant. He also received disability checks due to a heart condition. He preferred to work at night, and often worked all night and returned home at dawn to sleep all day.

As he grew up, he would hitch rides or catch the bus to get away from his rough neighborhood. Eventually, however, he still found himself in trouble. In November 1992, Ricky, now aged 34, was arrested for having fathered two children with a girl younger than fourteen. It was claimed that Ricky had been having sex with the girl since she was only eleven years old.

Ricky's public defender requested that the court grant Ricky a mental health exam. However he was found fit to stand trial. On September 1st, 1993, he pleaded guilty and was sentenced to jail. He ended up being released after thirteen months for good behavior. His relationship with the girl would not be his last lapse in good judgment.

Just before sunrise on June 15th, 1999, Ricky bought a one-way ticket to Orlando, Florida at the Greyhound bus terminal in St. Louis. No one knows who he met during his stay, but phone records show a large number of calls made to central Florida a couple of weeks before he arrived, made by both Ricky and his girlfriend, Sandra Jones. Ricky and Sandra made a similar amount of calls between them during the two days Ricky spent in Florida, and he made at least one call to the gas station where he worked.

Ricky was usually quiet about what he did during his trips to Florida, but this time when he returned, he was noticeably shaken and scared. He became even more erratic in the weeks following his return. Sandra has since reported to police she believes Ricky went to Orlando as part of a drug deal.

On the Day in Question:
On the afternoon of Tuesday, June 22nd, 1999, about a week after he returned from Florida, Ricky went to a hospital emergency room and complained of chest pains and shortness of breath. He had suffered from asthma and chest pains since childhood. He was

admitted for observation, and remained in the hospital for two days. After he checked out, Ricky visited his Aunt Gloria, leaving there in the late afternoon.

The next day, June 25th, 1999, at around 5pm, Ricky went to another emergency room, this time at Forest Park Hospital. He complained he was having trouble breathing after mowing the grass. This time, he was not admitted and was released at 5:50pm. Some report that Ricky spent the night in the hospital waiting room, but no one knows when he eventually left the hospital.

Sandra, Ricky's girlfriend, reports receiving a phone call from Ricky around 11:30am the next day. He said that he was on the way home and was stopping at the gas station where he worked to grab something to eat on the way. At least one gas station employee says they saw him that morning. That was the last time anyone reports seeing Ricky McCormick alive.

Ricky's body was found face down in a cornfield in a rural town in late June 1999. The cornfield was located in St. Charles County, twenty miles from St. Louis, where he lived and worked. Despite being only three days since his disappearance, his body already showed signs of significant decomposition.

The Investigation:
Due to the advanced decomposition of Ricky's body, police were unable to determine a definitive cause of death. However, they continue to suspect he met with foul play.

On December 23, 1999, an inter-agency meeting was called by the homicide department of the St. Louis

Metropolitan Police. Nine investigators attended, including those from narcotics, the Department of Housing and Urban Development, and an FBI special agent. At the meeting, it was reported that police were investigating a major drug dealer who operated where Ricky lived. Named Gregory Lamar Knox, he was a suspect in multiple homicides, including murder for hire. A police informant had told police that Knox had murdered a black man who worked at the gas station. However, despite stakeouts at the gas station, as well as the homes of several owners and employees, no arrest has ever been made.

Police interviewed Ricky's relatives, girlfriend and acquaintances, but nothing of substance was found. Soon, the leads began to dry up and the case was set aside.

Then, twelve years later, seemingly out of the blue, the FBI made a remarkable announcement. In March 2011, the chief of the FBI's Cryptoanalysis and Racketeering Records Unit announced that back when Ricky's body was discovered, police found two pages of handwritten notes stuffed into a pocket on his jeans. Although the individual letters used were the regular alphabet, the writing itself was not in any known language. The FBI had been unable to decipher their contents and they were releasing them to the public in the hopes that someone would be able to decode them.

At the time of his death, it was reported that McCormick could barely write his own name, and yet the papers found in his pockets had stumped the world's best code breakers. Typically, cases presented to this unit are cracked without a few hours.

Ricky's notes had remained unsolved for more than ten years.

Some have suggested that the letters are merely random scribbles, but the agent who worked on the case is quick to disagree. After examining the notes, he believes they are a true cipher and may hold important information regarding McCormick's activities just before he was killed, and possibly his murder.

Sifting through the deluge of information and theories provided by the public since the release of the notes, seven or eight possible leads have emerged. However, when followed up by the FBI or local law enforcement, nothing significant has ever emerged.

Suspects:
Police suspected Gregory Lamar Knox, a drug dealer who spent time near where McCormick lived. Knox was a suspect in multiple homicides, and had other criminal ties. The gas station where McCormick worked was also implicated, and had ties to Knox.

The original owner of the station had killed his neighbor with a butcher knife during an argument in his front yard in 1994. He died while serving a life sentence in prison. A man named Juma Hamdallah, a Palestinian immigrant, then took over the role of president of the business. He employed his brother, Baha Hamdallah.

However, the two had a rocky relationship. Within months of Ricky's death, police were called to an incident at the gas station, where Juma had allegedly shot Baha. Baha survived and no charges were filed.

However, the family has other violent ties. Another brother, Jameil, is a registered sex offender. But Baha is believed to be the most volatile, and has been involved in a number of physical altercations and even shootings.

Current Status of Case:
Both Gregory Knox and Baha Hamdallah eventually ended up in prison for other crimes. Knox pleaded guilty to possession with intent to distribute cocaine, and carrying a firearm. Baha Hamdallah was managing another store, when in October 2000 he got into an argument with a customer. Different versions of events have been presented in court, but the outcome was that Baha shot the customer in the face with a 9mm Glock outside the store. He was convicted of first degree murder. However, an appeal in 2006 granted a retrial, and in the second trial the jury accepted his argument of self-defense, and he was freed.

With little to now go on, investigators believe the only hope of solving the murder of Ricky McCormick is by deciphering his notes.

A Fatal Sleepover: Robert Wone

Victims: Robert Wone
Date: August 2, 2003
Location: The home of Joseph Price at 1509 Swann Street, Washington D.C.
Suspects: Joseph Price, Dylan Ward, Victor Zaborsky

Backstory:
Born in 1974, Robert Eric Wone was a lawyer from Fairfax County, Virginia. A graduate of the University of Pennsylvania Law School, he commuted to work in Washington D.C. Wone married his wife, Kathy Yu, in 2003. She also had a law degree from St. Louis University.

Wone was the first of two sons from a Chinese American family. He was a good student, and had graduated high school second in his class. At college, he participated in a club that was dedicated to anonymous good deeds, and while there, won an award from the school for good character.

After graduating, Wone studied law at the University of Pennsylvania. He graduated with honors in 1999, and he then clerked for a judge in the Federal Court in the Eastern District of Virginia. While working as a lawyer, Robert also did pro bono work for several organizations. He was president-elect of the Asian-Pacific Bar Association when he died.

Just a month before his death, Robert had gotten a new job as the general counsel for Radio Free Asia. After working late one night, and needing to be back at his desk early the next morning, he decided that rather than drive all the way home, he would stay with a friend in the city.

On the Night in Question:
On August 2nd, 2003, Wone was staying the night at a house owned by his friend Joseph Price and his partner, Victor Zaborsky. A third man, Dylan Ward, also lived in the townhouse, and (it was revealed later) was in a violent submissive/dominant relationship with Price.

Wone and Price were good friends, ever since they met while both attending The College of William and Mary. Like Wone, Price was also a lawyer and heavily involved in pro bono work. Being gay himself, the legal rights of gay families were of personal importance to Price.

Wone knew all three men, and they had even hosted his 30th birthday party at their townhouse.

Wone arrived at the home at around 10:30pm that night. His visit had been organized several days before. He had worked late and intended to stay over, rather than drive home to Virginia. By the time he arrived, it was claimed that Zaborsky was already in bed. It's reported that Wone hung out for a bit with Price and Ward. During this time, Wone briefly went outside. No one is sure whether he locked the door on his return.

Shortly after this, all three men retired to their rooms. Ward, who took a sleeping pill before bed, reported that he heard Wone showering in the bathroom down the hall.

Later, Price and Zaborsky reported that they were awakened by a security device that sounded when the house's door was opened. They didn't pay much attention, assuming it was their basement tenant returning home. Shortly afterwards however, they reported hearing a scream. They ran to Wone's room. They found he had been attacked.

Somewhere between 11:00 and 11:30pm, neighbors report hearing a scream. The scream was later identified as coming from Zaborsky. The scream also woke Ward. Zaborsky called 911, and paramedics were at the scene in just five minutes. The police arrived shortly thereafter.

Price also phoned Wone's wife. Wone was pronounced dead at 12:24am on August 3, at George Washington University Hospital.

The Investigation:
Police examined the scene, but found no evidence of a struggle. In fact, even the body itself was remarkably void of any blood. Though Wone had been stabbed three times, one wound almost big enough to be able to insert your hand, his clothing had only a small amount of blood on it, and there was none at all on the bed where he was lying. A towel that Price reported using to apply pressure to Wone's wounds had only a few small blotches of blood on it, rather than being soaked as one would expect with wounds of that size.

Later examinations would reveal that Wone had also been strangled, but it was the stab wounds that killed him.

All three residents of the house told paramedics that Wone had been attacked by an unseen intruder, but there were no signs of forced entry.

Forensics determined that Wone had been involved in a sexual act shortly before his death, whether willingly or not. His own semen was found on his genitals and inside his rectum. There were also multiple needle marks on his body, but nothing was found on a toxicology test.

A knife from the kitchen set was found by police on the bedside table. Price later reported that he had found the knife lying on Wone himself, and had picked it up and moved it to the side table. Was he accounting for his fingerprints on the knife? However, police do not think the knife found near the body was the murder weapon. Another knife from the set, with characteristics that better matched the murder weapon, was missing completely. The set belonged to Ward.

Both police and paramedics had already deduced that there was something that didn't sit right with the scene.

Wone slept with a mouth guard to prevent him from grinding his teeth, and this was in place. His wallet and watch were on the side table, and he was dressed in shorts and a t-shirt. Strangely however, he was lying on top of a made bed, and neither the bed nor his clothes had significant amounts of blood on them. As one of the paramedics would report, it looked as though Wone had been stabbed, then cleaned up, redressed, and put back on the bed. A police officer attending the scene noticed that all three residents of the house were dressed in white bathrobes, and looked as though they had recently showered, despite them reporting they had all been in bed at the time of the incident. All three were separated and interviewed by police for hours.

A detective noticed that Wone had typed emails to his wife and colleagues shortly after 11pm, but neither had been sent. Unfortunately, police later failed to copy the phone's hard drive before returning it to Wone's employer, and it was wiped before any evidence could be preserved.

Only forty minutes had passed between the time on the emails and Zaborsky's call to 911. How had the murder and cleanup happened so quickly, and so quietly, while three other people in the house supposedly heard nothing?

Multiple boxes of the three men's belongings were confiscated by police, and investigators also examined the house from top to bottom. They even removed parts of the floor and walls.

Blood evidence techniques found evidence of blood on the bed and throughout the room. However, authorities would admit later that the test reagent had been used incorrectly, and so no one could confirm whether what they found was in fact blood. The blood found on the knife at the scene was not consistent with Wone's blood. There was also no evidence of fabric from Wone's clothes left on the knife, despite him being stabbed through them. There were however, white cotton traces. Perhaps someone had wiped the knife with the bloody towel. Even more interestingly, a police cadaver dog found blood in a drain in the backyard, and also in a clothes dryer. Had someone recently washed bloody clothing in the house?

Suspects:
After another break-in at the house less than three months after Wone's death, Michael Price, Joseph's brother, came to the attention of police for Wone's murder. Michael had been implicated in the later robbery, and it was discovered that he had missed a class himself the evening Wone was killed. However, Michael's partner gave him an alibi and the police never arrested him.

There have been many theories regarding Wone's death. A detective suggested that the three were trying to make Wone join in on their three-way relationship, and he was murdered in relation to this. Others believe that perhaps Wone had been sexually assaulted by the men, or engaged in very rough consensual sex, where he died accidently or was killed to cover up an attack. However, any relationship between Wone and the three occupants of the house has been consistently denied. Other friends of Wone maintain he was heterosexual.

There have also been accusations of bias by Asian media, accusing the police of being afraid to accuse three white men for the killing.

After a year, the case was still unsolved. On the first anniversary of his death, a public appeal was made to find the killers.

The Trial:

In October 2008, Ward was charged with obstruction of justice. He had moved since the incident, and was now living in another home owned by Price, this time in Florida. In November 2008, both Price and Zabowsky were also arrested. Both men were charged with obstruction of justice. All three men were released while awaiting their trial, but they were fitted with electronic monitoring devices and given a curfew.

On December 19, 2008, additional conspiracy charges were filed against all three. During this hearing, the curfew and monitoring were removed; however prosecutors have announced that they may seek further charges related to tampering with evidence.

An affidavit filed by the authorities states that the investigation had determined that Wone was murdered after being sexually assaulted, and that there was overwhelming evidence that all three men had obstructed justice by cleaning and altering the scene of the crime by planting evidence, waiting to report the crime to police, and lying about the true details of the murder. All accusations were denied, and on June 29, 2010 all three were found not guilty by Judge Lynn Leibovitz in a bench trial. However, the judge stated in her ruling that she believes they know what happened to Wone.

In 2007, Wone's wife Kathy began a $20 million wrongful death lawsuit against Price, Zaborsky, and Ward. The suit was settled on August 3, 2011, for an undisclosed sum.

Current Status of Case:

Ward has since resettled back in Washington, and lives with Price and Zaborsky again. They have appealed to friends and family to help pay their legal bills.

Little Girl Lost: Caledonia Jane Doe

Victims: Jane Doe, real name unknown
Date: November 9, 1979
Location: A Farmer's Field in Caledonia, New York
Suspects: None

Backstory:
Caledonia Jane Doe, or simply Cali Doe, is the name that has been given to an unidentified murder victim found in Caledonia, in Livingston County, New York.

She was a young female, aged between 13 and 19 years old. She was found on November 9, 1979. Investigators believe she may have been from southern California, Arizona or perhaps northern Mexico. She had visible tan lines, suggesting she came from a sunny region.

The girl was estimated to be around 5 foot 3 inches tall, and weigh approximately 120 pounds. Her hair was brown, shoulder length and slightly wavy. It had been dyed blonde in the front about four months before her death. She had brown eyes.

Her teeth indicated that she had never received dental care. She had eaten a few hours before her death, and had been seen by a waitress in New York.

On the Day in Question:
A farmer in Caledonia saw red clothing in a cornfield on the morning of November 9, 1979. He thought that he had spotted a hunter trespassing on his land, but when he went to investigate, he found the body of a young girl. He called the police, and they were on the scene at 10:04am.

The girl was fully dressed, and her body showed no signs of sexual assault. The cause of death was two gunshot wounds. One was over her right eye, and the other was in her back.

Her pockets were all turned inside out, and if she had carried anything with her, including identification, it was now gone.

The Investigation:
An investigation of the scene revealed that the girl had likely first been shot on a road that ran alongside the field. A bloodspot was found there on the ground. She had then been shot again in the cornfield, after her body was dragged to its final position. Unfortunately, on the night of November 8, there had been heavy rains, and any potential evidence had probably been washed away.

Her clothes included a man's red nylon windbreaker, a boy's button up shirt, tan pants and blue knee socks. She did however wear female underwear, and jewelry.

In 2006, her clothing was tested for pollen or plant trace evidence. Pollen from Australian pine, oak, spruce, and birch trees were found. The pollen does not match the area where her body was found. The Australian pine pollen in particular is telling. It grows only in a limited number of locations in the U.S, including Florida, Texas, parts of Mexico, the University of Arizona and Arizona State campuses, plus three regions in California. The pollen would not have survived fall and winter where her body was found, and so the pollen had to have come from somewhere else. Investigators believe that the best pollen match comes from San Diego.

Although a murder weapon was never recovered, police believe it to be a .38 caliber handgun. A match to another gun or bullet used in other crimes has never been found.

Multiple truckers report seeing a girl matching Cali Doe's description hitchhiking just prior to the discovery of her body. One report puts her in Boston the night before she died. Another theory is that she was actually from Canada.

In 2005, her body was exhumed to extract DNA, in the hope that one day it will be matched to a living relative. Her teeth were also tested with isotope analysis, to try and determine where she grew up. The results indicate that she may have spent her childhood in the south or southwest region of the USA.

Suspects:
None.

Current Status of Case:
Due to the nature of the case, it has received wide media attention, and featured on such shows as America's Most Wanted.

Multiple composites of what she may have looked like alive have been made, but as of today Cali Doe remains unidentified.

A Senior Class Trip Tragedy: Natalee Holloway

Victims: Natalee Anne Holloway
Date: May 30, 2005
Location: Oranjestad, Aruba
Suspect/s: Joran van der Sloot, Deepak Kalpoe,
Satish Kalpoe,

Backstory:
Natalee Anne Holloway was a teenager from Alabama. She was a blonde haired, blue eyed beautiful girl, who embodied the all American girl. She was a straight A student, and well liked at her school. She had received a full scholarship to the University of Alabama.

During the final week of May 2005 she had travelled with 125 other members of her graduating class to Aruba for a week of fun. On the last day of the trip, only 124 teens gathered to return home. Natalee was missing.

On the Night in Question:
Natalee was last seen by friends at a popular nightspot around 1am the previous night. They witnessed her leaving in a gray Honda Civic with three unidentified young men. They shouted at her not to go, but she said she would be fine and left.

None of Natalee's friends or family have seen her since.

The Investigation:
Natalee's mother was notified by phone at 11am the next morning, and she immediately flew to Aruba with Natalee's stepfather George 'Jug' Twitty. They

claimed they immediately knew she had been taken, as Natalee had never been late in her life. Once they arrived, they started aggressively searching the island.

At first, their direct approach was successful in finding out the name of one of the boys Natalee had left with, Joran van der Sloot. He denied knowing her, but with the help of a sympathetic local serving as translator, he eventually admitted he had been with Natalee that night. He claimed that they had driven around the island in another friend's car. He, along with his friend, Deepak Kalpoe, and Deepak's younger brother Satish, had all driven Natalee around the island.

Joran claimed Natalee had been extremely drunk, and had given him oral sex. He claimed they had dropped her at her hotel, and had not seen her since. Due to the aggressiveness of the interview, the boy's father ended it soon after. Natalee's mother and stepfather returned to their hotel.

Natalee's family became increasingly pushy and involved in the investigation. They made remarks to the media that the authorities regarded as insulting towards Aruba. The Aruban investigators soon tired of Natalee's family. Her mother and stepfather threatened to 'bring hell to the island' if Natalee was not found.

As the case wore on, pressure to solve the case was placed on the authorities by the media and Natalee's family. At this time, Joran was put under intense pressure, and his story began to change. He now said that Natalee wanted to dance with him at the local restaurant, and pursued him when he refused. After she gave Joran a jelly shot, which she tipped onto herself for him to lick clean, they left in Deepak's car as originally reported. However, he now says that Deepak dropped him and Natalee at the Marriott Hotel and went home with his brother.

From there, Joran and Natalee allegedly fooled around on the beach, although they did not have sex. Joran reportedly refused because he did not have any protection with him. He claims that after some time he became tired, and told Natalee he needed to go. She then begged him to stay the night with her on the beach. After some teasing, he claims he eventually left her on the beach and called Deepak, who came and picked him up.

Joran claimed he and Deepak had failed to report earlier that they left her on the beach because he believed his father and friends would think badly of him doing so, plus he had a girlfriend.

In a twist to the story, a police report published by a local newspaper reported that Joran told police he believed Deepak returned to the beach on his own after dropping Joran at home. It was reported that police were told Deepak had killed Natalee and buried her somewhere on the beach. The newspaper editor did not release the names of the officers on the report, but was convinced it was authentic.

On June 29, 2005, Joran and both brothers were left alone in a police car, while unbeknownst to them the police recorded their conversation. During an argument, Deepak implied that it was Joran who should be worried if the police ever found Natalee, not himself. In the recording, Joran also threatened to kill Deepak.

Deepak denied ever returning to the beach, and cell phone records support his story. At this point Joran changed his story again. First he said he walked home from the beach. Then he said that although he called Deepak for a ride home, it was his brother Satish who picked him up.

Both brothers deny having anything to do with Joran after dropping him and Natalee at the beach that night. Computer records show Joran logged in at home at 3:25am. He sent a few messages to Deepak, visited sport and porn sites, checked his email and logged off around 4:30am. He was on the bus to school at 6:40am that morning.

In April 2007, Dutch investigators began to look at the case. A team of twenty forensic investigators searched and dug up Joran's parent's estate. They also searched the home of the Kalpoe brothers. To date, no further charges have been brought.

Suspects:
Several days after his initial interview with Natalee's family, Joran van der Sloot accused two black men who worked at the hotel as security guards. H said he had seen them approach Natalee when they dropped her off. Both men were arrested on June 5, 2005. Under Dutch law, the men could be held for up to 116 days with no charge.

However, Natalee's parents (by then her father had also arrived) were convinced that Joran and his friends were responsible, and continued to push police on this matter. On June 9, police arrested all three boys on suspicion of Natalee's murder. Four days later, the security guards from the hotel were released.

A man named Steven Croes was also arrested on June 17. He was a friend of Joran and Deepak, and worked as a DJ on a local party boat. He had backed up their story that the boys had dropped Natalee back at her hotel. Ten days later, a judge ruled that although Steven had lied to police, he wasn't involved in Natalee's disappearance, and he was released.

Soon after, on June 18 and 19, police questioned Joran's father for seven hours. He was a lawyer in training to become a judge. Four days later, the police arrested him also, but he was released without explanation on June 26.

On July 4, 2005 a judge released the Kalpoe brothers, but authorized police to hold Joran for another 60 days. The Kalpoe brothers were then arrested again on August 26, with police stating they had new evidence implicating them in premeditated rape and murder.

Six days later, the release of Joran was ordered. The next, the release of the Kalpoes was also ordered. Five days after that, Joran left Aruba to attend college in The Netherlands. It was now three months since Natalee disappeared.

In April 2006, Aruban police arrested a man they would only identify as G.V.C. He was revealed to be Geoffrey van Comvoirt, a 19 year-old former security guard who was allegedly involved in patrols along the beach at the hotel where Natalee was staying. He was released after six days of interrogation.

Another man with the initials A.B. was also arrested around the same time, but released after six hours. His name was never revealed.

The son of the Deputy Chief of Police was also briefly questioned.

In May, 18 year-old Guido Wever was arrested by Dutch police. He was a friend of Joran's, and worked at the Holiday Inn during Natalee's visit. He had left the island just two days after Natalee's disappearance. An extradition request was made by Aruba, but six days later Dutch police released Guido without charge.

Current Status of Case:
Beth Twitty, Natalee's mother, has been highly critical of the handling of the case. Her attitude has alienated nearly every sympathetic contact she had in Aruba. There are reports of her stepfather physically attacking an Aruban reporter in the lobby of the hotel. The Deputy Chief Gerold Dompig has publically stated that pressure from Natalee's family forced the arrest of Joran and the brothers too early, and had damaged the investigation. He stated pressure from as far up as the White House in America was too much for the country, who relied so much on their image in the USA for tourism income.

The editor of the newspaper who published the police report remains convinced that Joran and the Kalpoes are the guilty parties. He states that Joran had access to several boats, and could have used one to dispose of the body. He believes Natalee was most likely killed at Joran's apartment on his parent's estate, a one-acre property surrounded by high walls. He believes that Joran's father helped the boys in the aftermath, and coached them on what to say to police.

Natalee's mother, Beth, has since divorced from her second husband. Rumors have surfaced that she is dating John Ramsey, the father of JonBenet Ramsey.

Natalee's family filed wrongful death suits against both the van der Sloot family in New York and against the Kalpoes in California. Both were dismissed. The Kalpoe family also filed a suit against the *Dr. Phil Show* for defamation, as a result of an interview with Deepak on the show. They claim the show was edited to make it seem like Deepak claimed he had sex with Natalee, when in fact the unedited version has him denying it.

In 2008, a video emerged that had Joran van der Sloot talking to a friend. He claimed that he and Natalee had sex on the beach, and afterwards Natalee had a seizure. He claimed he called a friend, and the friend helped him dump the body in the ocean. However, the tape was not proven to be sufficient evidence to re-arrest Joran, and a warrant request based on the taped 'confession' was denied. Joran, who was smoking marijuana during the recording, claims he was under the influence and what he said on the tape was a lie.

Joran has since told the media in 2008 that he sold Natalee to people smugglers for $10,000, and then in

2009 that he dumped Natalee's body in a marsh, rather than the ocean. Shortly after the second 'confession', Joran's father died of a heart attack. The Chief prosecutor maintains that neither of Joran's statements are at all credible, and do not match known facts.

However, there has been one final twist in the story. Five years after Natalee's disappearance, on May 30, 2010, Joran was in Peru to participate in a poker tournament. There, he was captured on hotel surveillance video taking a Peruvian woman named Stephany Flores Ramirez to his room. Four hours later, he left alone, and two days later Stephany's body was found by housekeeping. She had been bludgeoned to death.

A warrant was quickly issued for Joran's arrest, and through an Interpol warrant, he was arrested outside Santiago, Chile. Meanwhile, on July 3, 2010, Joran was charged in Alabama with extortion and wire fraud, which allowed the United States to request his extradition. It was claimed that Joran tried to extort money from Natalee's mother, offering to reveal the location of her body. Dutch authorities searched his home on July 4, acting on behalf of the F.B.I.

It was announced on July 7 that Joran van der Sloot had offered a confession to the killing of Stephany Flores, but in such a way that it would result in a manslaughter charge, rather than murder. His mother has expressed concern that the confession was coerced, and he tried yet again to retract his confession. However, it was ruled by a judge that the confession was valid, and Joran eventually pleaded guilty to her murder. He was sentenced to 28 years jail.

In June 2011, Natalee's father filed a petition to have her legally declared dead. Natalee's mother announced her intent to oppose the petition. A hearing was held on September 23, 2011 and it was ruled that the conditions for a legal presumption of death had been met. On January 12, 2012, in a second hearing Judge King signed the order declaring Natalee Holloway to be dead.

Conclusion

These are only some of the murders that remain unsolved. The murders attributed to Jack the Ripper, the Jon Benet Ramsey case and the Lizzie Borden murders all remain open. History provides us with case after case of unsolved murders and it will certainly continue to do so.

Dear Readers

Thank you for purchasing this book. I enjoyed researching and writing about these cases and I hope you found them to be both interesting and engrossing.

If your friends and family would enjoy reading about this topic, please be sure to let them know about this book.

Again, thank you for your support and I look forward to writing more books of Murders Unsolved.

Regards,

Mike Riley

Be sure to check out Mike's other books:

Hollywood Murders and Scandals: Tinsel Town After Dark
"In the late afternoon, her friends recalled, Monroe began to act strangely seeming to be heavily under the influence. She made statements to friend Peter Lawford that he should tell the President goodbye and tell himself goodbye."

More Hollywood Murders and Scandals: Tinsel Town After Dark
"At some point in the night Reeves and Lemmon began to argue. As Reeves headed upstairs to his

bedroom, Lemmon would later tell officers that she shouted out that he would probably shoot himself."

Made in the USA
Lexington, KY
25 November 2018